"Deeply rooted in biblical references, this new book for religious leaders in this post-modern world could serve as a catalyst in a church to face a new future. One strong feature is inviting the reader to reflect on one's own blind spots and biases that contribute to the resistance for change. Besides bravely acknowledging today's challenges, Jones and Fredrickson in the end offer ways to become more aware of reality such as the Examen Prayer, spiritual direction and the Quaker clearness. For the Christian faith to continue, trusting in God's plan along with a new model of leaders who are 'inwardly directed and outwardly focused' may give us hope."

—Don Ng, former president of American Baptist Churches, USA

"Where is the primary focus of your congregation? Is it in the past, present, or future? *Being Church in a Liminal Time* guides congregations through a discernment process, providing provocative questions to assess their capacity for, "Remembering, Letting Go, and Resurrecting." This is a question that every congregation in the U.S. should be asking themselves."

—C. Jeff Woods, general secretary, American Baptist Churches, USA

"The Church's need to embrace brave change is clear—but how? Technical changes called forth by the pandemic have not addressed the deeper transformation required. The authors do not offer us a book full of strategies; rather, as in the parables of Jesus, we are presented with stories and fundamental images, deep reflection upon which can offer us a path forward towards the resurrection which is our hope."

—The Rt. Rev. Alan M. Gates, bishop, Episcopal Diocese of Massachusetts

"In and through this book Jeffrey Jones and David Fredrickson offer the Christian churches a bountiful gift. Certainly, it is my hope that it will be seen and received in this way for what they put forward here is nothing less than a careful and honest assessment of the current Church landscape and the presentation of three guiding images and a new model of leadership that could redirect congregational life in bold new ways in this seemingly liminal time. I highly recommend this book to all who still care about the present state and potential future of the Christian churches."

—Benjamin Valentin, professor of theology and Latinx studies, Boston College School of Theology and Ministry

"Dave Fredrickson and Jeff Jones have written an insightful book about the church in America today. This is a backdrop for my story and that of many others I meet. I left a church that had nurtured me and prepared me to walk out the door, a church where I had served as a Sunday school teacher, youth group leader, and lay leader. I crossed the road, not far, but a world away from my small suburban church, a church more "Remembering" what had once been. I went to the inner city and became part of an Urban Youth Ministry in one of the poorest and most violent cities in America. I call it my church today, twenty years later, no longer angry at the Church, I now meet the most amazing people who serve alongside me and most all come from the Church 'Resurrecting.'"

—Jim Cummings, director of experiential learning at UrbanPromise Ministries

"Reading motivational books can make a huge difference in how one sees him or herself and the world around them. I was struck by the personal inner focus on the three images of remembering, letting go, and resurrecting. The imagery of a loved one journeying through hospice care and the church's strategic planning response through its membership decline stage helped me to appreciate the relevancy of this book. It draws you toward proactive assimilation and forces the reader to examine how to do Christ's commission inwardly and outwardly, with precision, at the same time. I strongly encourage this book for ecumenical and Christian small group discussion."

—Lois B. Wilkins, African American Cultural Resource Center (AACRC) chair, Betty J. Johnson North Sarasota Library, Florida

BEING CHURCH IN A LIMINAL TIME

Remembering, Letting Go, Resurrecting

JEFFREY D. JONES AND

DAVID FREDRICKSON

AN ALBAN BOOK
ROWMAN & LITTLEFIELD
Lanham • Boulder • New York • London

Published by Rowman & Littlefield
An imprint of The Rowman & Littlefield Publishing Group, Inc.
4501 Forbes Boulevard, Suite 200, Lanham, Maryland 20706
www.rowman.com

86-90 Paul Street, London EC2A 4NE

British Library Cataloguing in Publication Information Available

Library of Congress Cataloging-in-Publication Data
Names: Jones, Jeffrey D., author. | Fredrickson, David, author.
   Title: Being church in a liminal time : remembering, letting go,
      resurrecting / Jeffrey D. Jones and David Fredrickson.
   Description: Lanham : Rowman & Littlefield, [2023] | Includes
      bibliographical references and index. | Summary: "In a time when the old
      answers about being church no longer work and new answers are not yet
      clear, this book offers a way forward to help congregations live more
      faithfully. It suggests three guiding images that help congregations
      both understand their current reality and deepen their engagement in the
      ministry to which God has called them"-- Provided by publisher.
   Identifiers: LCCN 2023007332 (print) | LCCN 2023007333 (ebook) | ISBN
      9781538174494 (cloth) | ISBN 9781538174500 (paperback) | ISBN
      9781538174517 (ebook)
   Subjects: LCSH: Church renewal. | Mission of the church. | Christian life.
   Classification: LCC BV600.3 .J655 2023 (print) | LCC BV600.3 (ebook) |
      DDC 262.001/7--dc23/eng/20230503
   LC record available at https://lccn.loc.gov/2023007332
   LC ebook record available at https://lccn.loc.gov/2023007333

Holy Saturday

Holy Saturday is the time

- after death, before resurrection
- when the old has gone and the new has not yet appeared
- a liminal time, a time betwixt and between

It is a time

- of grief and uncertainty
- of loss and waiting

During this time there are

- days we feel abandoned
- days we feel paralyzed
- days it is difficult to have hope

It is a time for praying.

Contents

ACKNOWLEDGMENTS

Writing a book is never a solo project—or in this case a dyadic project. We are grateful for the many conversations we have had with many people about the direction and content of this book.

The first thoughts that led to the writing of this book came as we were co-teaching two leadership courses at Andover Newton Theological School. The students in those courses asked probing questions, shared deep hopes, and provided keen insights into ministry that stimulated our thinking and started our writing.

Dwight Stinnett, Dean Allen, and Tina Walker-Morin all read the manuscript and offered comments that were both insightful and encouraging.

Randy Van Osten, Mayra Castaneda, and Daryn Bunce Stylianopoulos shared stories of their ministries that enhanced our understanding of church life and possibilities for the future of the church.

Over the past several years we have had the privilege of participating in a Zoom group that provided a community of sharing and caring that sustained us during the pandemic and offered continuing encouragement for our work. We are deeply grateful to Wes Bixby, Brett Opalinski, and Hovnan Demerjian for their friendship and presence in our lives.

Editors, even supportive ones, have a difficult job. The effectiveness of their work depends upon their ability to critique. But they need to do this without being negative and in a way that enables the writers to hear what is being said. Beth Gaede is an excellent editor! She was with us almost from the beginning as the book moved through several different formats and emphases. And she did the final edit of the manuscript. Her input made the final product a much better book.

Dave wants to thank his wife Johnna and their two boys Colin and Jared for their support and encouragement throughout the writing process.

Jeff's wife, Judy, knows what writing a book does to a person and his (in the case) relationships with others. He offers his thanks to her once again for her patience, encouragement, and insight.

Chapter 6 is based on material from Robert Quinn, *Change the World: How Ordinary People Can Accomplish Extraordinary Results* (San Francisco: Jossey-Bass, 2000). We deeply appreciate his generosity in granting us permission to make use of his work.

INTRODUCTION

It's clear that deep and profound changes are taking place in the world and the church. Congregations are caught in a maelstrom of change with all the tension, uncertainty, fear, and dislocation that brings; they are struggling to find an appropriate way to respond. The impact of those changes has been written and talked about for decades. Congregations, with the support and encouragement of denominational leaders, have tried countless ways to reverse the decline these changes have precipitated. One can easily question why yet another book about congregational response to change needs to be written. But the truth is that despite significant effort expended on a vast array of strategies, the struggle and decline continue. There is a growing realization in congregations, denominations, seminaries, and other religious institutions (at least of the North American mainline variety) that established patterns of worship, Sunday school, congregational structure, denominational programming, clergy preparation, and just about everything else have not been able to respond to the challenges of the time in a way that returns the church to its previous position of influence in society.

Even the profound dislocation caused by the COVID-19 pandemic did not bring significant and deep change in congregations. To be sure, at the height of the pandemic, the delivery system changed, and congregations had to move to providing virtual experiences. But what was being delivered changed very little. The church continues to do what it has always done, now just with a hybrid or virtual approach rather than an exclusively in-person approach. The same style of worship, the same form of Bible study, the same approach to fellowship, the same board and committee meetings have continued—just in a hybrid or virtual form.

While the switch to virtual and/or hybrid formats entailed a major effort, it has been a technical change, not a deep one. Perhaps these changes will make the need for deeper changes apparent in the future, but so far this deeper change has not materialized, and for the most part we don't even know what it might be.

Given the myriad attempts at change, the abundant resources that have been devoted to them, and the lack of any significant, long-lasting results, it seems reasonable to conclude that something different is needed.

Barbara Brown Taylor describes our predicament this way:

> The way many of us are doing church is broken and we know it, even if we do not know what to do about it. We proclaim the priesthood of believers while we continue living with hierarchical clergy, liturgy, and architecture. We follow a Lord who challenged the religious and political institutions of his time while we fund and defend our own. We speak and sing of divine transformation while we do everything in our power to maintain our equilibrium. If redeeming things continue to happen to us in spite of these deep contradictions in our life together, then I think that is because God is faithful even when we are not.[1]

Susan Beaumont in *How to Lead When You Don't Know Where You're Going* describes this time as a "liminal season."[2] The old answers about what congregations are to be and do no longer work, but the new answers are not yet clear. It is life in the in-between that leads to uncertainty, frustration, and fear. In a sense, all times are liminal because change is a constant, but this time is especially so because there are many forces at work to disrupt the way things have been. There seems to be no solid ground on which to stand.

HOW TO READ THIS BOOK

While clear answers aren't possible in a liminal season and even partial answers vary from one context to another, guiding images can provide a beginning point for exploring and discerning. This book presents three such images: remembering, letting go, and resurrecting. In fact, most congregations operate out of at least two of these images already even if they are not aware of it. One is typically the dominant, or formative, image. This is the image that exercises the greatest influence in shaping the congregation's life and ministry. As we explore these three images, keep in mind that we are not advocating one as the "true and faithful" image for all congregations. It isn't that one of the images is right and the others wrong or even that there is one "best" image every congregation should adopt. All three have the potential to enable faithful ministry for a congregation. The challenge to congregations, however, is to acknowledge the image that shapes its identity and minister out of that awareness, while still seeking to grow in faith and faithfulness. Here's a preview of the journey we'll be taking in the pages ahead.

Chapter 1—A Reality Check: The demise of Christendom, with its alliance of church and state/culture, is a major precipitator of the liminality congregations are experiencing. It has caused the church to lose many of the supports that once assured the regular flow of people and finances. A Bible study of the parable of the sower is used to reflect on the realities congregations face as they seek to respond to this time. While this parable leads us to confront the reality of death, it also reminds us that during great change God is doing a new thing and calling us to get involved.

Chapter 2—Possibilities for the Future: Because of the rapid and radical change taking place in the world, every institution needs to make a fundamental choice between deep change and slow death. Deep change requires letting go of much of what currently exists. Since dying is an essential aspect of both deep change and slow death, it is important for congregations to be grounded in a resurrection faith. To help them do that, this chapter includes a Bible study process for use with 1 Corinthians 15:12–28. One way to be open to the possibilities of the future is to consider a simple question: What is God up to and how do we get on board? A congregation's answer to this question is not shaped by just one image. Rather, the images are combined in a variety of different ways to shape the unique identity of each congregation. One image usually has greater influence, but in most cases all three images are present.

This chapter describes ways in which the images are at work in various congregations.

Chapter 3—Remembering: Although there is much to cherish in the ministry of traditional congregations, this is often lost sight of in concerns about declining numbers and fewer financial resources. Many congregations include people whose families have been members for generations, and they have deep and cherished memories of the church, its past leaders, its ministries, and the building. Difficulty in facing the decline and possible demise of a cherished institution often makes denial a powerful factor in the life of these congregations. However, even if a congregation is unable to face the possibility of its death, it can still have a significant ministry, acting faithfully to do the right thing in its time and place. It may provide the continuing nurture and support needed to sustain the life and faith of those for whom traditional ways of being church are essential. It may provide comfort amid the turmoil of a changing world. It may provide a community of acceptance and friendship. While accepting the potential for significant ministry even when denial is strong, this chapter also explores ways in which a congregation might lessen the need to deny.

Chapter 4—Letting Go: If a congregation can recognize the reality of decline, accept that there is little chance of reversing that trend, and admit the probability of its death, it can let go of dimensions of its life and ministry that are no longer viable. This chapter will explore the insights that hospice care can provide for a congregation that has accepted the likelihood of its eventual death. A brief description of hospice care as it is practiced for individuals is followed by a process for use in a congregation.

Chapter 5—Resurrecting: A dying church can provide a way into the future and a new way of being church. This chapter offers a Bible reflection on the parable of yeast (Matthew 13:33) to provide insights into a possible new expression of church. A faith community shaped by this image is grounded in the love of God and guided by the way of Jesus. A survey of communal disciplines offers insights for being grounded in God's love. A reflection on Luke 4:16–22 offers insight for claiming the ethic of Jesus.

Chapter 6—A New Model of Leadership: Inwardly Directed and Outwardly Focused: The church in this liminal time, regardless of its guiding image, needs leaders who see and act in new ways. This chapter provides a framework for considering an approach to leadership that is spiritual and responds to the realities of liminality. Each element of the framework is explained, with biblical and practical illustrations and suggestions for both individual and group exploration. This way of leadership takes great personal strength coupled with profound sensitivity to others.

FINAL THOUGHTS BEFORE WE BEGIN

There are no easy answers to the questions and challenges facing the church in today's world. Our hope is that the insights provided in this book will lead you to affirm the ministry of your congregation and recognize what that faithful work means for the present and the future.

Before we begin it is essential for us to acknowledge the limitations of our work. Some of those limitations arise out of our experience, which has primarily been in predominantly white, mainline congregations. This doesn't mean that what we have to say applies only to congregations similar to those where we have worked, but it is a reminder that we do not have the experience to speak directly to all the expressions of the church in today's world. This acknowledgment brings us to our hope that this effort may in some way encourage a conversation among those of us involved in and committed to the church to live and minister more faithfully.

One final note about terminology: In order to speak about the church in general and specific institutional expressions of the church without confusion, we will use the following nomenclature: "church" refers to the church in general and "congregation" refers to the specific institution that exists and in which people participate. We recognize that many readers customarily use other terms, such as parish or church, for that specific institution in which they are involved, but this seems to us the simplest way for us to explain what we are talking about.

Notes

1. Barbara Brown Taylor, *Leaving Church: A Memoir of Faith* (San Francisco: Harper-Collins, 2006), 220.

2. Susan Beaumont, *How to Lead When You Don't Know Where You're Going: Leading in a Liminal Time* (Lanham, MD: Rowman & Littlefield, 2019), 1–22.

CHAPTER 1

A Reality Check

Living in the In-Between

As he came out of the temple, one of his disciples said to him,
"Look, Teacher, what large stones and what large buildings!"
Then Jesus asked him, "Do you see these great buildings?
Not one stone will be left here upon another; all will be thrown
down."

—MARK 13:1–2

THIS IS A BOOK ABOUT DISCERNING WHAT GOD IS ABOUT IN THIS LIM-
inal time and how we can become a part of what God is doing. The challenge before us is significant. We believe that the days of the institutional
church as we have known it are coming to an end. In fact, the pandemic
that began in 2020 may have accelerated its demise. Many congregations
that exist today won't be around in twenty years. That painful reality is
impacting the life and ministry of all existing congregations. It is painful
for us, just as it must have been painful for the disciples to hear Jesus's
words with which we began this chapter.

A NEW THING
The pain of this reality can easily lead to frustration and a sense of hope-
lessness. But there is good news for us, even now. In the midst of the
current struggle, uncertainty, and grief, God is at work doing a new thing,

redeeming the old, and leading us to greater faithfulness. God is always about that, and this is always good news. As is often the case, the struggle itself might be God's way of getting our attention and calling us to action. All too often we hesitate, though, because a new thing necessitates the passing away (dying) of the old. We resist the death of the way of faith we cherish; we fear the loss it will entail; we grieve the demise of the way things used to be. Neither of us denies this, and we'll talk a good bit about it, but our focus will be on what we can do to live more faithfully. We believe Dietrich Bonhoeffer had it right when he noted, "Christianity conceals within itself a germ that is hostile to the church. It is far too easy for us to base our claims to God on our own Christian religiosity and our church commitment, and in so doing utterly to misunderstand and distort the Christian idea."[1] Christianity does conceal within itself a germ that is hostile to the church. Our challenge is to discover that germ and the reason for its hostility and then to find a way to embody God's new enterprise more fully.

As Barbara Brown Taylor has noted, it is the faithfulness of God that makes it possible for people of faith to maintain hope when so much of what we are familiar with is unraveling, when the old is passing away, and when we cannot be at all clear what the new will be. In such a time it is vital that we keep trying to understand the reality we face as we also seek to discern the promise the present holds. We do that recognizing that no one, certainly including us, will get it completely right, but all of us have something to contribute to the discussion. It is in that spirit and hope that we make our contribution.

This is part one of our reality check: God is doing a new thing and calling people of faith to be engaged.

THE END OF CHRISTENDOM

There are many reasons for the state in which congregations and other religious institutions find themselves. This part of our reality check will deal with one of these. We believe some of the most significant and helpful insights come from an understanding of the church's inability to respond in a meaningful way to the demise of Christendom. Since the reign of Constantine in the fourth century there has been some form of alliance between the church and state. Sometimes it has been political, at other times cultural, but, in the West at least, it has always been there, and the church has depended upon it. In a very short time following Constantine's victory at Milvian Bridge in 312 CE and the Edict of Milan in 313, the church moved from being an illegal outsider on the margins of society to being one of the most powerful institutions in society. The state began to advocate for and support the church, enforcing its beliefs and helping it to solidify its doctrines. The church, in turn, became the legitimator of the state. Thus, the Council of Nicaea, which produced the Nicene Creed, was called and presided over by the emperor, who wasn't a baptized Christian, for the purpose of developing a set of common beliefs that could be used to unify the Empire.

Later, kings, queens, and other rulers imposed their particular expression of Christianity on their subjects, again to enhance political unity. This, in turn, led to conflict, bloodshed, and wars, as states with different religious expressions battled each other. In North America, the Puritan attempt to build a "city on a hill" in New England was based on a close alliance of church and state, with church membership an assumed requirement for public office and clergy taking an official role in civic affairs. The colony depended on the state's willingness to use imprisonment, torture, genocide, and execution to support specific religious and civic beliefs.

Later still, in the United States, blue laws were enacted to support and protect the practices of Christianity. In many schools children, no matter their faith, began the day with the Pledge of Allegiance and the Lord's Prayer. The American flag assumed a prominent place in sanctuaries as the church continued its support of an American civil religion that provided a basis of unity in the political realm. Then, during the 1950s, as some feared the alliance was beginning to weaken, Congress adopted "In God We Trust" as the official United States motto and required that it be printed on all currency (seemingly not recognizing the irony involved). At that time Congress also added the words "under God" to the Pledge of Allegiance.

The extended trajectory of that alliance has now created an expression of "Christianity" that seeks to use the forces of the state to enforce a rigid authoritarianism based in a primary loyalty to a program of Christian nationalism that advocates for cultural and racial exclusion. In this case, some segments of the "church" have been co-opted by a political movement seeking support for its ideology.

At the same time there was a growing reliance in the church on secular thinking and methodologies to shape its worldview and practice. Early on the church adopted the structure of the Roman army as a model for its hierarchy. It continues today with church leadership that relies on secular perspectives on management, marketing, control, and change. This has led to a loss of the unique worldview of the gospel and its insights. Alan Roxburgh, seminary professor and founder of the Missional Network, in his book *Joining God in the Great Unraveling*, puts it this way:

> While there is now a recognition that something is terribly wrong, the dominant structures and narratives of the modern project (power, method, solution-driven fixes) remain so entrenched and so powerful that these churches are, literally, dispossessed of their own stories and imagination as God's people. The Christian tradition is mostly a vague memory when it comes to addressing the anxiety and fragility of our time rather than the vital force discerning what God is calling us into. Too many congregations and their leaders are unclear about how to distinguish between the narratives of the modern project and the Christian story. This is continually illustrated in the kinds of tactics that get adopted to address the unraveling.[2]

The alliance with state and culture that Christendom provided served as a prop for congregations, helping to ensure a steady flow of members and the financial support they brought with them. As we noted earlier, beginning in the mid-twentieth century in the United States the alliance began to erode. The 1962 school prayer decision of the Supreme Court is perhaps the best illustration of this. In that decision, the Court ruled that it is unconstitutional for state officials to sponsor the recitation of prayer in public schools. The trend has continued: attendance in a church is no longer an entrée to the country club or a prestigious job, sports compete with worship, clergy no longer have the prominence and influence in the community they once had. Christendom is over as far as the secular world is concerned, but its aura still exercises significant influence within the church. As long ago as 1991, Loren Mead, former president of the Alban Institute, noted in his book *The Once and Future Church:* "We are surrounded by the relics of the Christendom Paradigm, a paradigm that has largely ceased to work. But the relics hold us hostage to the past and make it difficult to create a new paradigm that can be as compelling for the next age as the Christendom Paradigm has been for the past age."[3]

The church (at least the Western, mainline church) faces an array of new challenges today because the state and/or cultural support upon which it depended for 1,700 years no longer exists. This is a significant reason for the decline congregations are experiencing. It is also why attempts to respond to that decline—renewal, revitalization, and transformation efforts—have failed. The relics of the Christendom paradigm have had a more powerful hold on us than most of us realize. Mead's insight, while acknowledged, has yet to be heeded in any significant way. These relics continue to shape the thinking of even many of us who imagined we understood and believed we were challenging that paradigm. They continue to cause us to yearn for a time when status and influence will once again belong to the church and its clergy. They continue to shape an understanding of what the results of renewal should be. The more radical implications of the demise of Christendom have not become operating assumptions for congregations or the church as a whole. Most renewal/ revitalization/transformation efforts are still measured by quantitative criteria, such as membership and budgets, that judicatories so diligently collect. These criteria are based on institutional assumptions about the church that may have been valid in Christendom but are no longer. They encourage a continuing focus on reclaiming members, financial stability, and influence, which were marks of success in the Christendom church. To be fair, perhaps the church doesn't know any other way to be, but this focus has directed efforts away from the change that is needed to respond to the new realities of a post-Christendom world. And so, our attempts at renewal have by and large been misdirected, which is why they have been unsuccessful.

For the most part, congregations involved in renewal efforts measured by these criteria are seeking resuscitation; they are attempting to bring the body back to life in the same form and with the same qualities it had at the height of its prominence. The deep change needed, however, requires a major reorientation in what it means to be Christian and what the church is to be and do. The realities of the post-Christendom world demand an entirely new understanding of what success is and the way in which it needs to be measured. They require, as Bonhoeffer suggested, paying attention to the germ that exists within Christianity that is hostile to the church and what the church has become. When congregations do that they might then be able to face the new realities of the present and even let go of much that has been a part of the church in the past. They might then be able to die to much of what has been. Resurrection, not resuscitation, is what is needed. This resurrection may come, in some cases, as existing congregations discover a new way of being once they accept decline and eventual death. In other cases, it will come as new forms of church begin to emerge.

Again, Roxburgh offers an important insight for us on the "unraveling" he sees taking place in society and the church and the inability of both to enter a process of "reweaving." Contemporary religious organizations, he says, are "driven by technique," attempting to use a never-ending array of new programs and strategies to solve problems of declining membership and finances. "Their primary concerns are about how to make their church successful," and they have "defaulted to methods of management where prediction and control are high values." They are "clergy centric, driven by a professionalized, ordained class from whom the congregation expects direction." He also notes that these characteristics taken together "reveal a more critical deformity driving these churches: the primacy of human agency."[4] All of this negates the possibility of being attentive to the Spirit and focusing on ways God is already at work in the neighborhood.

We believe this is the reality the church faces today. And yet, there is even more to it. Having said all of this, because God is always at work even when we don't see or acknowledge it, congregations that remain steadfast in the way things have always been as they seek resuscitation might still minister in meaningful ways, touching those whose lives and faith are nurtured in traditional ways. This also is a foundational premise in our thinking and of this book.

This is the second part of our reality check: The Age of Christendom is over.

The Parable of the Sower

With this as background, let's move to the third part of our reality check and think a bit about what it means for you in your congregation. To do that we offer this Bible study based on the Parable of the Sower. As we ponder this parable, we will make use of Old Testament scholar Walter Brueggemann's helpful insight about the prophetic use of metaphor. In times when the old ways no longer suffice and new ways are needed, imagination is essential. It takes creative imagination to begin to envision what God might be up to. Brueggemann suggests that the value of a metaphor is not that it provides a one-to-one correspondence between its parts but rather that it "proceeds by having only an odd, playful, and ill-fitting match to its reality, the purpose of which is to illuminate and evoke dimensions of reality which will otherwise go unnoticed and therefore unexperienced."[5] Our aim will be to use playful imagination to develop a deeper understanding of the present and a more profound hope for the future of the church. We'll be using metaphor throughout the book to explore significant issues and concerns. Our hope is that this will enable us, as Richard Rohr, founder of the Center for Action and Contemplation, has written, to be "holy fools," neither seeking to conserve nor react against the past, but "to let go and let God do something new on earth."[6]

A sower went out to sow. And as he sowed, some seeds fell on the path, and the birds came and ate them up. Other seeds fell on rocky ground, where they did not have much soil, and they sprang up quickly, since they had no depth of soil. But when the sun rose, they were scorched; and since they had no root, they withered away. Other seeds fell among thorns, and the thorns grew up and choked them. Other seeds fell on good soil and

7

brought forth grain, some a hundredfold, some sixty, some thirty. (Matthew 13:3–8)

This parable is about the reign of God. And yet, while it addresses an eschatological concern, it also speaks to contemporary realities and the renewal attempts that seek to reestablish a presumed "successful" past. Perhaps the parable's most striking aspect comes with the realization that there is a lot of death here! The seeds that fell on the path died as they were eaten by the birds. The seeds that fell on rocky ground produced plants that quickly died. The seeds that fell among thorns produced plants that also died. Following Brueggemann's insight, a playful use of imagination suggests a perspective from which to consider the many efforts at congregational renewal that have been implemented during the past several decades. Congregational renewal efforts have become big business, and yet after all the effort and expense, not much has changed.

A large percentage of these efforts have not produced the results that have been expected. The birds snatched the seeds of renewal before they could even take root. The failure of results might be from an inability to agree on what to do, or perhaps the resources to do anything just weren't there. Whatever the reason, nothing happened, the seeds promising new growth never took root, and there was nothing to show for the effort that had been expended. Perhaps it went something like this:

> The new priest at St. John's Parish had many ideas. She had taken several congregational renewal courses in seminary. She had attended every workshop she could that offered new ideas for leading change and was committed to the denomination's program of congregational transformation. This was one of the reasons the search committee had decided to recommend her to be their new priest and the reason the vestry supported that decision. She knew, of course, that the process would be slow, that she couldn't simply tell the congregation what to do and how to do it. But she was confident that applying what she had learned would produce the results she hoped for and the congregation's leaders said they wanted.

Her plan was to begin with a brief but broad study that looked at the overall state of congregations in North America—their challenges, their potential resources, and ways to decide on a course of action. A dozen people showed up for the first session. They had a lively discussion and it looked like the process was underway. But at the second session, only seven people showed up. Calls to those who didn't return revealed several reasons, including family events and schedule conflicts, but no promises were made to attend the next session. The three people who showed up for the third session decided it probably wasn't worth continuing at this time. Everyone was just too busy.

To say that all renewal efforts fail, however, would be inaccurate. Over these years, many congregations have planted seeds of renewal that have taken root and produced results. But, in many cases, they have not produced lasting results. Many of the congregations that adopted renewal strategies gained new members but began to experience another decline within just a few years after the growth spurt. The renewal had no depth so, like the seed on rocky soil, it withered away. Their story might have gone something like this:

First Church was a 150-year-old congregation in a small city. It had a long history of involvement in the community and had maintained a worship attendance of about one hundred through most of the middle of the twentieth century. Some noted that just maintaining the same worship attendance at a time in which the city was growing significantly did not bode well for the congregation, but it seemed to most people that there was no reason for worry. Then a lay leader of the congregation committed a violent crime. This led to a significant decline in membership. Within a few years worship attendance averaged between forty and fifty, and the congregation could only afford a part-time pastor. A new pastor arrived, who brought both energy and creativity to the congregation. Worship became livelier through his preaching and a revitalized music program led by a dynamic

9

young musician. The congregation was agreeable to all the changes and appreciated most of them. Gradually worship attendance increased from about forty to between fifty-five and sixty. There were budget concerns and a few differences of opinion on issues, but the congregation weathered all these storms. The increased worship attendance brought a greater ethnic diversity to the church, which led the pastor to suggest at a church council meeting that it might be good to consider the possibility of changes in worship and other offerings of the church to respond to that diversity. He noted that it would likely be difficult to sustain the involvement of new attendees unless more was done. One member of the council observed that since the new people were coming now, they must like worship the way it is, so there was no need to change. That comment was greeted by silence. The topic was never raised again, despite efforts of the pastor to engage the congregation. Within a year average worship attendance was once again forty.

In still other congregations over the years the seeds of renewal have sprouted, but the changes have not been easily accepted. Sometimes these changes have been strongly opposed by members who were set in their ways, and other times they required too much effort to maintain. Time after time, those who advocated for change became disillusioned by the lack of support and left. These and other responses often led to controversy and conflict. The thorns of exhaustion, frustration, or conflict choked the renewal efforts. More than one congregation had an experience similar to this:

Immanuel Church had talked for fifteen years about hiring an associate pastor. Somehow it had never been the right time, or the resources just weren't there. So, it never happened, even though it was still talked about as something they would do someday. When it came time to call a new pastor, the church decided on someone who would help realize this dream rather than focus on the pastoral calling that had been the strength of the previous pastor. The new pastor brought change to worship, with preaching that no longer focused primarily on personal concerns. He no longer consulted with the informal group of longtime members who had made many decisions in the past, relying instead on established boards and committees. New members were elected to office to join the long-term members. New programs began to be introduced. Within two years worship attendance had grown 20 percent, giving was up 30 percent, church membership up 10 percent, and a local seminary student was hired as the associate pastor with the expectation that she would remain after graduation.

Soon the complaints began: the new pastor didn't visit as the previous one had, the new pastor used a smaller group of people to make decisions, the new pastor couldn't get along with the staff, the new pastor was making commitments the congregation might not be able to fund in the future. Then, at an annual meeting, one of the older members announced to the congregation that there was a significant level of dissatisfaction in the congregation and moved that a committee be established to evaluate the current ministry of the church. After some discussion the motion passed. Seeking to avoid conflict, the official church leadership was reluctant to challenge the complaints, and so they festered. The church decided not to make a commitment to fund the associate pastor position, so she left after graduation. After another year of effort to overcome the resistance to his leadership, the pastor resigned. Within ten years the church had only a half-time pastor.

Questions for Reflection:

- In what ways has your congregation been "sowing seeds"?
- If you had to pick one "seed experience" that best describes the experience of your congregation, which would it be?

- What new insights about your congregation and its experience of dying does this reflection raise?

- As you read the three illustrations, consider how they might relate to your congregation? Are there elements in these stories that are similar to your story? Does one story capture more of the experience of your congregation? If you were to write your story, what would it be?

Let's continue our "playful encounter" by considering ways in which the soil that is key to the parable might be interpreted in the three stories. For some reason, the specific contexts did not enable the hoped-for changes even though seeds were sown. There was no growth because the soil did not enable the seeds to take root deeply enough to be sustained. So, what made the soil inappropriate? To some extent the problem might have been the specific culture of an individual congregation—the resources available to it, the leadership, the sense of community, the support available from the judicatory, the unwillingness of the congregation to accept the need for change, changing demographics in the surrounding neighborhood, economic factors such as the closing of businesses in the surrounding area. All these factors, and countless others, could have contributed to the failure of these seeds of renewal to flourish, hence making slow death inevitable.

But we can also think about the soil as the array of broader societal and cultural factors at play. We have looked at the demise of Christendom as one significant factor, but there are others. The development of postmodernity with its suspicion of structure, its questioning of universal truth, and its celebration of diversity has had an impact on every institution, as has the rise of social media and the rapid and constant emergence of new technology. More recently the COVID-19 pandemic has forced changes upon every congregation. The setting in which the church finds itself—the cultural soil into which the seeds of renewal have historically been sown—is radically different from what it was just a few decades ago. These seeds cannot produce lasting results in this cultural soil as they did in the previous soil. So, now the question is, might we need to change not the soil (because that cannot be changed) but the seed? Could it be that the seeds we have been sowing are for the wrong kind of plant—a plant that could thrive in the previous soil but not in the current one? Additionally, might the seeds based in technique, management, marketing, strategy, and control that work well in a secular environment be the wrong seed for the church? There's no easy or simple answer to these questions, but the parable provokes us. It leads us to ask questions and seek new insight.

Questions for Reflection:

- What are the major societal and cultural ingredients that make up the "soil" in your setting?
- What impact do they have on the life of your congregation?
- How do these impact your ability to change?

The seed that fell on the good soil and produced phenomenal growth leads us to even more significant questioning. Certainly, the abundance provided by these seeds is the "happy ending"—growth and renewal—for which congregations engaged in renewal efforts hope. It seems to be an affirmation of the power of God at work. It appears to be an assurance that even if many efforts fail, we will be successful if we continue to work at it—if we sow enough seed. But truth be told, there's death here, too. For the grain to grow, the seeds that fell on the good soil had to die. New growth was possible only because the seed that was sown died. Put another way, the seed didn't produce a larger seed, it produced something radically different, but only because it died. Jesus stated it clearly: "Unless a grain of wheat falls into the earth and dies, it remains just a single grain; but if it dies, it bears much fruit" (John 12:24).

Now this parable leads us to consider what death is needed today to produce abundant results and also what those abundant results might be. Are we willing to let things that are important and meaningful to us die so new growth can take place? None of us is eager to do that.

Rustin E. Brian, Senior Lecturer of Theology at African Nazarene University in Nairobi, Kenya, and an adjunct professor at Northwest

Nazarene University, in his book *The Death and Resurrection of the Church* provides a helpful insight:

> We must give up our obsession with growing large, significant and powerful, or anything else grandiose and instead we must simply desire to be faithful, accepting along the way that our numbers will be fewer, our power and influence will wane, and the features that we've taken for granted as normative for church structure and polity for so long will go away.[7]

Alan Roxburgh also suggests aspects of congregational life that need to die:

> The almost automatic, default response [to the unraveling occurring in congregations] is the production of methods borrowed from other disciplines that might offer techniques for managing change. There is little recourse to asking how we practice a discerning of God's agency rooted in Christian tradition. It is more natural, for example, for congregations and denominations to embrace methods of strategic planning, helping people, adaptive change, innovation, marketing, consumer analysis and so forth with little sense that something is profoundly absent in all this taking on of the modern and its methods.[8]

As with most attempts to predict what the future will offer, these insights may not be totally correct. They do, however, illustrate possible deaths that will lead to the resurrection of the church. We can discover what those deaths are only if we are willing to ask difficult questions and consider radical and new ways of thinking and acting.

Questions for Reflection:
- How do you respond to the notion that the dying of old ways of being the church is needed today?
- How do you respond to Brian's and Roxburgh's statements regarding current aspects of congregational life that need to be let go?

This is the third part of our reality check: The dying of old ways is inevitable.

AN IN-BETWEEN TIME

For the fourth and final part of our reality check we return briefly to the insight of Susan Beaumont about the liminal season we are experiencing that we shared in the introduction. Much of what we have said so far in this reality check deals with the demise of the old and the need for the new. That is an important aspect of our current reality, but that is not the full picture. A liminal season is always much more complex.

A liminal season is an in-between time. The old is passing away but not completely gone. The new is emerging but not fully present. Old ways continue, and some need to be accepted. New ways are being developed and need to be encouraged. People who depend on the old ways are still here and need to be supported and encouraged in their faith. People who seek new ways are here and need to be supported and encouraged in their faith.

This is why we think it is vital to affirm a great variety of ways of being church in these days. The old is important. The new is essential. Neither is more faithful than the other. God does not honor one approach and condemn the others. In the next chapter we will begin to explore a way of recognizing and encouraging three different approaches to being faithful in this liminal season.

Here ends the reality check!

NOTES

1. Dietrich Bonhoeffer, "Jesus Christ and the Essence of Christianity," in *The Bonhoeffer Reader*, edited by Clifford J. Green and Michael DeJonge (Minneapolis: Fortress, 2013), 68.

2. Alan Roxburgh, *Joining God in the Great Unraveling* (Eugene: Cascade, 2021), 48.

3. Loren Mead, *The Once and Future Church* (Lanham, MD: Rowman & Littlefield/Alban, 1991), 18.

4. Roxburgh, 13.

5. Walter Brueggemann, *Cadences of Home: Preaching Among Exiles* (Louisville: Westminster John Knox, 1997), 1.

6. Richard Rohr Daily Meditation, "Wisdom: Becoming Wise Fools," February 26, 2021, https://cac.org/daily-meditations/becoming-wise-fools-2021-02-26/.

7. Rustin Brian, *The Death and Resurrection of the Church* (Eugene: Cascade, 2021), 31.

8. Roxburgh, 48.

CHAPTER 2

Possibilities for the Future

Discerning an Image of the Congregation

God of grace and God of glory, on Your people pour Your power.
Crown Your ancient church's story, bring its bud to glorious flower.
Grant us wisdom, grant us courage for the facing of this hour.
—HARRY EMERSON FOSDICK

IN HIS BOOK *DEEP CHANGE*, ROBERT QUINN, A MEMBER OF THE FACULTY of the University of Michigan business school, maintains that because of the rapid and radical change that is taking place today, all institutions must make a fundamental choice between deep change and slow death. There are no other options. Deep change is "major in scope, discontinuous with the past, and generally irreversible."[1] For our purposes, deep change necessitates letting go of much of a congregation's traditions and structure. This letting go is, in fact, a form of death—a dying to old ways of thinking and acting. Undergoing deep change requires a willingness to risk not knowing what the outcome will be. It is a great challenge that many congregations are not able to meet. The only alternative, according to Quinn, is slow death, which often includes many years of frustration and decline. However, it is our belief that, even during the process of slow death, it is possible for a congregation to face that it is slowly dying and offer significant ministry to its members and beyond if it chooses. Through the grace of God, even when a congregation avoids facing the reality of slow death, it can still provide meaningful ministry. Whether in a process of deep change or slow death, death is inevitable. But just as certainly, God is present and at work.

While this talk of dying may sound depressing (even fatalistic) to some, as people of faith we come to our discussion of the inevitability of death with an awareness of resurrection. Assurance of the resurrection helps us face the reality of death. Even as individual congregations die, they participate in the resurrection of the church as a whole. Because resurrection is a key to our discussion it will be helpful before we go further to reflect on one of the classic New Testament passages about the essential nature of Christ's resurrection. Although all of 1 Corinthians 15 provides significant food for thought, we'll focus on verses 12 to 28:

> Now if Christ is proclaimed as raised from the dead, how can some of you say there is no resurrection of the dead? If there is no resurrection of the dead, then Christ has not been raised; and if Christ has not been raised, then our proclamation has been in vain and your faith has been in vain. We are even found to be misrepresenting God, because we testified of God that he raised Christ—whom he did not raise if it is true that the dead are not raised. For if the dead are not raised, then Christ has not been raised. If Christ has not been raised, your faith is futile and you are still in your sins. Then those also who have died in Christ have perished. If for this life only we have hoped in Christ, we are of all people most to be pitied.

> But in fact Christ has been raised from the dead, the first fruits of those who have died. For since death came through a human being, the resurrection of the dead has also come through a human being; for as all die in Adam, so all will be made alive in Christ. But each in his own order: Christ the first fruits, then at his coming those who belong to Christ. Then comes the end, when he hands over the kingdom to God the Father, after he has destroyed every ruler and every authority and power. For he must reign until he has put all his enemies under his feet. The

last enemy to be destroyed is death. For "God has put all things in subjection under his feet." But when it says, "All things are put in subjection," it is plain that this does not include the one who put all things in subjection under him. When all things are subjected to him, then the Son himself will also be subjected to the one who put all things in subjection under him, so that God may be all in all.

In this passage Paul was addressing those in Corinth who had doubts that the resurrection of the body applied to them. They seemed to accept the belief that Christ was raised from the dead but had not been able to connect that to belief in their own experience. So, Paul was arguing that the two are integrally linked together. The focus of the passage is personal resurrection, but there are hints in the phrase "put all things in subjection" that Paul sees the experience of death and resurrection extending beyond the individual to all creation. This thought is made explicit in Romans 8:22, where Paul writes that "the whole creation has been groaning in labor pains" as it, along with us, waits for redemption that comes through resurrection. In Ephesians 1:10 Paul again speaks of God's "plan for the fullness of time to gather up all things in him."

We'll use the passage from 1 Corinthians as a takeoff point for considering ways in which resurrection may apply to the experience of congregations. Here are some thoughts that might provoke your own thinking and conversations with others:

- Paul maintains that the resurrection is the key to the Christian faith.

- Paul insists that Christ's resurrection and ours are intimately tied together, that it is impossible to have one without the other.

- Paul asserts that without a resurrection that applies to all people, not just Jesus, the Christian faith has little meaning.

- Paul indicates that resurrection is for "all things," not just personal life after death.

- Paul encourages the Corinthians to live their lives with faith in resurrection.

- Paul believes that this faith gives us reason for hope in this life and the life beyond.

As you consider these thoughts, reflect on the following questions, either personally or in a group discussion. Rather than attempting to answer all of them, you might want to select those that touch issues most significant for you or your congregation.

- In what ways might these insights relate to death and resurrection as it applies to the church and to your congregation?
- Jesus has said that not even the gates of hell will prevail against the church (Matthew 16:18). In what ways does a belief in resurrection support this promise?
- In what ways do these insights on resurrection offer hope while letting go of what has been important in the church and your congregation?
- How might the resurrection provide reason for hope in the midst of what seems to be declining church membership and resources?
- How might the resurrection impact your response to the decline and ending of traditional aspects of the life of your congregation?

With faith in resurrection, we can speak even of death with hope. This doesn't mean there is no loss. It isn't an antidote to pain and sadness. It doesn't eliminate the need to grieve. But it does mean that death does not have the final word. And it affirms Jesus's promise that not even the gates of hell will prevail against the church. Many congregations and many traditional ways of being church will die, but there will also be resurrection for the church. Rustin E. Brian, in his book *The Death and Resurrection of the Church*, says it well:

> In many ways, I believe the current model or form of the church in North America is dying. Perhaps this is a good thing? . . . I would point out the core of the gospel: resurrection. Ours is a God of resurrection. And resurrection comes only after and

through death. . . . My contention is that much of the church, like you and I—all of us—will die. So, too, though, will the church be raised to new life in Christ.[2]

DISCERNING THE RIGHT THING

So, what is a congregation to do in this liminal time when old ways and forms are dying? In the discussions that eventually led to this book, we authors struggled with that question. Congregations are being pulled in many directions. There are so many offerings, so many strategies for change or renewal or growth. Somehow, we knew we wanted to cut through all that and offer something different, something more helpful. We knew it couldn't be simple, but we hoped it could be genuine. During that struggle, we were struck by an insight from Margaret Wheatley, management consultant and writer, in her book *So Far from Home*. In it she made what we thought was a startling confession. Although not in her words, this is the essence of it: I used to think I could save the world, but now I understand the world is so messed up I can't, so what I need to focus my efforts on is doing the right thing in the setting in which I find myself.[3] That rather shocking admission provoked our own thinking about the church. We realized quite quickly that given the ongoing decline most congregations have experienced in both people and resources, the inability of congregations to reverse that decline despite significant efforts, and the lack of any compelling new form of church, we could make a similar statement about the church. It would go something like this: We used to think we could change (renew, revitalize, transform) the church, but now we realize the church is so messed up we can't, so what we need to do is focus our efforts on doing the right thing in the setting in which we find ourselves. From our perspective Wheatley's attempts to change the world were based on a reliance on technique, management, and control that have been unable to bring about the needed change.

We have come to realize that the complex realities we have been discussing are clear indications of a "messed up" church. Operating out of deeply embedded assumptions about what a congregation should be doing too often leads to a persistent focus on institutional maintenance and survival rather than God's work in the world—slow death, not deep change. Those who serve in leadership positions are too easily burned out. More than a few leaders have ended their terms of office by withdrawing from church life altogether. Following the assumptions of the Christendom model of church, we have created an institution that all too often makes it impossible for people to do the very thing the church is supposed to do, namely, the will of God. It has become exceedingly difficult for the contemporary congregation to be a community that facilitates spiritual growth and deeper engagement with God, one another, and the world. Instead, all too often, it has become an institution that manages a building and a budget, offers programs of interest, and provides ongoing support and validation for a way of life that is culturally, economically, and politically appropriate.

Wheatley's notion of simply doing the right thing offers a new possibility for us. It suggests that we move away from a process of decision-making to one of discernment—from what *we* want to accomplish, the hopes *we* want to realize, and what *we* have always done to focus instead on being part of the right thing in the place we happen to be. It's not about us choosing our future from the possibilities that we see but discerning God's best future for us. Our hope is founded in something far different than results, for hope based on anticipated results is always a false hope. Thomas Merton reminds us that our basis for hope is strongest when it does not depend upon the results that we expect:

> Do not depend on the hope of results. When you are doing the sort of work you have taken on . . . you may have to face the fact that your work will be apparently worthless and even achieve no results at all, if not perhaps results opposite to what you expect. As you get used to this idea you start more and more to concentrate not on the results but on the value, the rightness, the truth of the work itself.[4]

This is a hope grounded in simply discerning and being part of the right thing. We believe a laser-like focus on doing the right thing is what will enable each congregation to discern its way of being. So, what is this "right thing" we are to be about? There are many ways to express it, of course, none of which is exhaustive or captures the whole truth. For us, discovering the right thing is about exploring and discerning an answer to a rather simple question that Jeff posed in a previous book: What is God up to and how do we get on board?[5] It's a simple question, but asking it doesn't lead to an easy answer. We cannot continue to believe that old assumptions about what congregations do will provide an answer. We cannot simply look to the experts to answer the question for us. Neither can we look to the past and the answers it offers. We can't simply explore what others are doing.

Discerning an answer to the question "What is God up to and how can we get on board?" points us to the "right thing." It requires us to reorient ourselves in a way that opens us to be attentive to the Spirit's presence and willing to follow the Spirit's leading, even as it asks us to let go of much we assumed was the answer in the past. We cannot do this by developing a new strategic plan. We cannot do it by seeking to implement the changes we want to see happen in the congregation. It can only happen when we are ready, personally and institutionally, to set aside our own preferences, wishes, and hopes so that we can discern the work God is about in the world and how the Spirit is showing us the way to join in.

The right thing can be something radically different from what currently exists. It will forgo much that has been assumed to be essential to the church in the past. It will continue to change and evolve. Specific expressions of it may come and go. This is what will enable deep change so that a new form of church can emerge.

The opposite may also be true, however. The right thing may be continuing to do the many things that have always been done by a congregation in order to provide a community for those whose faith is tied to long-practiced traditions. But these things can be done with a new perspective. These things can be done not with the expectation that if they are done right, growth in members and finances wilzl inevitably happen. Rather, they can be done to provide a ministry of love, support, and service for those who find these qualities through familiar patterns of ministry. In this case, the right thing will look very much like the old thing, but it will be done knowing that while it may not bring growth in the way it was once hoped, it is the thing God is up to in that setting.

Finally, a congregation may be about the thing God is up to without acknowledging the reality of its eventual demise but continuing to do what it has always done for as long as it can. This can still be the right thing because God is at work even when we do not see the way in which that work is being done. Just by continuing to do the old things this congregation may well be providing the place of acceptance and faith that sustains and supports, while also avoiding direct acknowledgment of the likely death that is too painful to face.

THREE IMAGES

It is this awareness that there are a variety of ways for congregations to engage in ministry during this liminal time that led us to name three images that capture the formative mindset of congregations. While the congregations can be radically different from each other, God is at work in and through all of them. They can all be places of love, acceptance, mission, and justice. All can be about the "right thing" for their context. All too often resources about congregational renewal/revitalization/transformation have implied (if not directly asserted) that congregations that do what they suggest are on the right track, while those that do not are somehow wrong or unfaithful. That's not what we are about. We believe God is at work in congregations regardless of their formative image. Because of God's faithfulness to the church, good things can happen, sometimes even without our planning or awareness.

These are the three images we use to describe in a broad way the possible responses a congregation might make to the question. What's God up to and how can we get on board?

- Remembering—This image sees God at work among those who were nurtured in the ways of the traditional church and continue to receive support for their life and faith through them. It cherishes the past and is devoted to maintaining traditional ways in its ministry to people who rely on them. It is likely, however, that congregations that adopt this image will continue to decline and eventually close.

- Letting Go—In many ways this image results in an expression that is similar to the congregation whose guiding image is remembering. It seeks to minister to those who were nurtured in and still find support in the traditional ways of the church, but it also sees God at work in the forming of new expressions of church and, because of this, recognizes that there is a limit to the institutional viability of traditional forms of church. It recognizes the need to face the reality of impending death and to respond to that reality.

• Resurrecting—This image is based on an understanding of God at work in the movement beyond traditional ways of being church and seeking new forms and structure, including those that bear little similarity to existing congregations. It is exploring and experimenting, seeking to discover a new way to help shape the church that is emerging.

We have intentionally used the word "image" because there is a looseness to it. It doesn't suggest a specific form, structure, or style of ministry. Rather, it offers a way for a congregation to define itself and discern its path into the future. No congregation is shaped by just one image, however. Rather, the images combine in a variety of different ways to provide the unique identity of each congregation. One image usually has greater influence but, in most cases, all three are present. We have called the dominant image formative in that it has the greatest influence in forming the congregation's life and ministry. The two secondary images also play a role, but with less influence.

To get a handle on the way this works, here are three imaginary descriptions of congregations whose life and ministry are shaped by each of the formative images, followed by an analysis of the way in which the images are at work in each.

WHEN THE IMAGES COMBINE
Remembering—Main Street Church
Main Street Church was once the predominant congregation in the town. Several members of the town council were active in the church, as were numerous local business leaders. The youth group attracted children who attended other churches on Sunday morning but came to Main Street's youth group on Sunday evening. The stable population in the town meant that there were several two- and three-generation families who were members. The church had a long history of capable pastors who were excellent preachers. Even as mainline congregations began to

decline, this reputation of good preaching enabled the congregation to sustain both its membership and its finances.

The growth that characterized the 1950s and 1960s didn't continue, but there was no apparent decline until the 1990s. When a new independent church opened just outside of the town, several families joined that congregation, saying that they liked its more contemporary worship style and exciting youth programs. Main Street Church's decline continued as older members retired and moved away or died. The town's youth soccer program began to schedule games on Sunday morning, which meant families with children who participated became less and less regular in their attendance. Add all this to the general decline that was taking place in most congregations and, in what seemed like no time at all, attendance was only half of what it once had been. Although financial contributions to the congregation had declined along with membership, the endowment was being used more and more to fund the budget and maintain the staff and programming. The longtime members who made up most of the congregation talked fondly about the days when the sanctuary was full, the choir was large and well known for its excellence, and an array of age-level programming was well attended. Even as it became necessary to curtail some programming and eliminate raises for staff, they still talked about the need to return the congregation to the position it once held in the community.

Members consistently pressured the pastor and other leaders to do something that would attract new members. They were convinced that if they found the right program and worked hard enough to implement it, the days they remembered could become a reality again—if not completely, at least enough to maintain the congregation's presence and influence in the community. They believed this is what God wanted and if they would just do things the right way, it would happen.

The formative image of Main Street Church is remembering. The congregation focuses on the way things were in the past and maintains the hope that a semblance of the past can be theirs once again. This focus on remembering means denial of the inevitability of decline and the reasons for it are strong. While the congregation has had to end several meaningful programs, it still hasn't let go of them, as it continues to hope to revive them at some point in the future. Similarly, while it has had to adapt to the new reality it faces, there has been little or no intentional desire to make lasting changes, maintaining the hope that much of the past can be revived. The images of letting go and resurrecting have little influence in this congregation. However, while shaped by the image of remembering, the congregation still provides a meaningful ministry to those whose faith was formed and is sustained through these experiences.

Letting Go—Trinity Church

Trinity Church is in a small city about fifty miles from a large metropolitan area. It was founded in the nineteenth century and has had a continuing ministry to the city ever since. Its building is an impressive structure on the main street. Following World War II the congregation experienced significant growth, leading to the addition of an expansive education wing in the early 1960s. From that time into the 1980s the congregation experienced a balanced stability in both membership and finances. There was no significant growth, but also no reason for concern about the viability of the congregation. Its program and ministry continued in much the same way as it had for thirty years.

By the late 1980s the signs of decline were beginning to show. Worship attendance began to decrease, the youth group no longer thrived or attracted youth from throughout the town, and it was becoming increasingly difficult to fund the staff and program through the annual stewardship campaign. At first the change was barely noticeable and attracted little attention. By the late 1990s, however, the decline was becoming increasingly obvious. Several church growth programs were implemented with little success. The congregation explored different styles of worship, but these did not attract new people and the current members were not comfortable with them. In the early twenty-first century a controversy over a social issue developed, causing several families to leave, increasing the rate of decline. More and more people began to ask what would become of Trinity Church. As the anxiety built, the decline continued, despite efforts to reverse it.

When a new pastor arrived in 2015 the congregation was ready to consider the possibilities for its future, realizing that things could not continue as they had in the past. As they began to consider the future, they developed an extensive list of possible scenarios. When this was shared with the congregation, there was general agreement on only one option—no one wanted to continue as they were and do nothing. The congregation entered a series of reflective discussions with three groups: with themselves to share their own hopes, wishes, and prayers for the future; with three declining congregations each of which had chosen a different option for its future; and with leaders and social service organizations in the city to learn more about the needs that were present and how the congregation might respond to them. Although all members were invited to join these conversations, only a small group participated in all of them. As the group considered all the options it became clear that the best one would be to close but retain some type of presence in the community. This was shared with the entire congregation. While there was sadness, nearly everyone understood and accepted the rightness of the decision.

The formative image of Trinity Church is letting go. They have determined that there is little hope for the congregation's long-term survival. Their desire to negotiate the continuing decline involves gradually letting go of the way things used to be, as well as considering what that means for the ministry that will continue until the closure occurs. Remembering and resurrecting will each influence this process. The remembering will help them prioritize various aspects of their ministry to determine what to continue. Resurrecting will enable them to shape a different way of being even as they move to the time of closure. The process of letting go has begun, but they have not yet developed new ways of being. As this process continues, they will be providing a ministry to those who have been a part of the congregation, as well as those they have ministered to through their mission efforts. They will also be able to consider how their remaining resources will be used.

Resurrecting—Faith Church

Faith Church is located on the main street in a small town not far from a large metropolitan area. It is one of four mainline congregations in the town, along with several independent congregations. Into the first decade of the twenty-first century it was in many ways a typical established mainline church offering traditional worship and educational experiences, but it was also reluctant to consider the way the world was changing and what that could mean for its life and ministry. Since that time, it has experienced significant decline and uncertainty.

In 2016 the congregation took the risk of calling a pastor who in many ways was very different from those of past decades. The hope was that a different style of leadership and ministry would help the congregation respond more faithfully to the realities it faced. Among other things he began a second service shortly after he arrived that was more contemporary and interactive. It was going well and attracting new people until the pandemic came, and everything fell apart. His approach in this crisis was to gather a group of people to do a building use study, which was the beginning point for a number of significant changes. The former fellowship hall became the town thrift shop and food pantry. A nonprofit organization was formed to provide community services, including weekly dinners. The nonprofit receives funds from the United Way to support its activities. These ministries have become a major point of service to the community. They have also attracted a significant number of people who are not members but who volunteer to help with the various projects. They see the need for what is being done and want to support it. This has brought another dimension to the ministry of the congregation as it develops relationships with the volunteers who are not likely to ever be members. These ministries have become an important force in the town for meeting the needs of people. This service emphasis is grounded in a Sunday worship experience that brings an ongoing spiritual dimension to all the church does.

The formative image for Faith Church is resurrecting. They have faced the reality of their situation and have let go of much of what they have done in the past. Although they see the need for significant change, there is a passion to maintain and expand ministry to the community. They have taken steps to repurpose much of the building and developed new entities that can provide more effective service.

They are not certain where this will lead but have a commitment to ministry in their neighborhood and to reaching as many people as they can, including those who volunteer. As they continue this process, they will be remembering what they have been in the past, discerning what elements of that can be present in a different form and setting. They will also be letting go of much of the former life and ministry of the congregation. There may be little in the future that looks familiar, but responses to the needs of the community will continue to emerge in new forms.

The diagram below depicts the three images in each corner of the triangle. If a dot were placed in the center of the triangle that would represent a congregation in which all three images exercised the same influence in shaping the life and ministry of the congregation. A dot in one of the corners would represent the congregation's exclusive use of that image. The reality in most congregations, however, is that one image predominates and the other two have less influence. That reality is pictured by the placement of a congregation somewhere within the triangle closest to its formative image and in relationship to the other two images according to the influence they have. The congregations described above have been placed in the diagram to illustrate this.

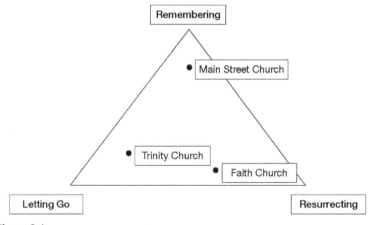

Figure 2.1

As you consider the interplay of the images in your congregation, determine where you would place the congregation on this diagram. If you are working with a group, ask the members to work individually on this and then share and compare the results with each person explaining the reasons for their placement. Once there is a consensus about the formative image, it will be possible to use the material in the related chapter to enhance the congregation's experience with that image. Remember, it is not a matter of being right or wrong, faithful or unfaithful. Congregations with all three formative images have the potential to offer significant ministry in this liminal time, each responding to different people with differing needs in their spiritual journeys.

No matter how the images come together, all three types of congregations fall short of establishing the reign of God on earth. They are all imperfect human institutions that are hampered by human foibles and sin. Because all three fall short of the glory of God, they each have the potential to move to a fuller expression of the reign of God. That movement will be one of our concerns throughout the book.

THE INEVITABILITY OF LOSS

Loss is an inevitable part of this process of finding and doing the right thing. Not everything the church has done in the past is the right thing for this time and context. If we are to grow in faithfulness, we will need to let go of these things. It will be necessary for us to grieve their loss, to acknowledge that we miss them, to admit it is painful to give up cherished ways. This is true even if we trust that God is about resurrection for us and for the church.

The current reality for the church is one of great uncertainty. That's how it always is in liminal times of unrelenting change. We have a sense that the old is passing away and have little awareness of what the new will be. But amid this uncertainty, we can affirm that God is at work to redeem even what might seem to us to be hopeless causes. We can also affirm that even in our uncertainty there are ways to be faithful to God's call and the Spirit's leading. That faithfulness can and will take different forms but, no matter the form, it can contribute to the emergence of the future that God has in store for the church and all creation.

Congregations that continue in traditional ways provide a setting for vital ministry to and with those whose faith has been and continues to be shaped and supported by its ways—and yet this form of church is most likely not sustainable. This is true whether or not the congregation itself recognizes and accepts the likelihood of its slow death—whether its formative image is remembering or letting go. When the formative image is resurrecting, much will be radically different, without many of the attributes that have been considered essential to the church in the past—and yet no one knows what precise form this will take. All are essential and legitimate forms of church in this time.

Brian McLaren, in *Faith After Doubt*, talks about his hope for a church in which congregations are "communities of faith expressing themselves in love."[6] We believe this provides a good description of congregations that have found the right thing for them to be about. These congregations may take different forms in different settings but, at its core, the right thing is about faith expressing itself in love. All three types of congregations have the potential to express themselves in love. They will express their love in different ways. None of them can be communities of faith expressing themselves in love all the time. But when they are striving to be this, the "right thing" is being done, and they have joined in the work that God is doing.

NOTES

1. Robert E. Quinn, *Deep Change: Discovering the Leader Within* (San Francisco: Jossey-Bass, 1996), 3.

2. Rustin E. Brian, *The Death and Resurrection of the Church* (Eugene: Cascade, 2021), 12.

3. Margaret Wheatley, *So Far from Home: Lost and Found in Our Brave New World* (San Francisco: Berrett-Koehler, 2012), 4–7.

4. "Thomas Merton's Letter to a Young Activist," https://jimandnancyforest.com/2014/10/mertons-letter-to-a-young-activist/.

5. Jeffrey D. Jones, *Facing Decline, Finding Hope: New Possibilities for Faithful Churches* (Lanham, MD: Rowman & Littlefield, 2015), 67–78.

6. Brian McLaren, *Faith After Doubt: Why Your Beliefs Stopped Working and What to Do About It* (New York: St. Martin's, 2021), 137.

CHAPTER 3

Remembering

A New Way of Seeing What Was

I consider the days of old,
and remember the years of long ago.

—PSALM 77:5

THERE IS MUCH FOR CHRISTIANS TO CHERISH IN THE MINISTRY THAT traditional churches once had and, in many cases, still do have. Unfortunately, many often lose sight of this by fretting about declining numbers and fewer financial resources. The situation is much like that conveyed by the psalmist in Psalm 77:7–9:

> Will the Lord spurn forever
> and never again be favorable?
> Has his steadfast love ceased forever?
> Are his promises at an end for all time?
> Has God forgotten to be gracious?
> Has he in anger shut up his compassion?

It is in remembering that the psalmist begins to find reason for hope again. This psalm is an affirmation that God is still at work no matter how bad things seem. The key to this affirmation, of course, is to begin to discern the way in which God is at work and how to become a part of that. Or, in the words of our question: What is God up to and how can we get on board?

Congregations whose formative image is remembering (what we have called remembering congregations) are struggling with this challenge of seeing what God is up to now. Many of these congregations include families who have been members for generations. They have deep and cherished memories associated with the congregation, its past leaders and ministries, and the building. Current leaders often feel a sense of obligation to maintain the congregation in traditional ways and would consider an inability to do that as a failure on their part. These forces combine to make it difficult, if not impossible, for the congregation to face the possibility that the decline it is experiencing will eventually lead to death. Denial is a powerful factor in the life of these congregations. It serves to protect them from a painful reality when they do not have the spiritual resources to face it. In most cases this denial cannot be confronted directly. However, if there are those who do understand, it is possible to avoid enabling the denial and lead members of the congregation to a point where they are more able to face it.

Memories of past events and people have a powerful impact for congregations in which remembering is the formative image. There may be memories of previous pastors and their preaching or caring, a filled sanctuary, the leaders of the town or city who were once members, the large youth group the congregation once hosted, or anything else that was a sign of the importance the congregation had in the lives of members and the community. Some of these memories are real, others may be exaggerated or even false, but they are all powerful. A focus on these memories often results in a desire to recapture these experiences in the hope of re-creating the time of influence and status the congregation once had. Congregational renewal and church growth strategies offer a promise of this return, so congregations often devote significant time and resources to them, usually without the success they hoped for. But the memories remain strong and continue to shape the congregation's identity in a way that makes it all but impossible to think of being anything else.

In this chapter we'll look at the meaningful ministry these congregations can still have, despite all the changes that have taken place. We'll also explore ways in which it might be possible to encourage more meaningful engagement with the realization that they are focused primarily on the past and are seeking to re-create it.

Dave's childhood congregation was the epitome of the remembering congregation. The church closed several years ago after 150 years of ministry to the community. Dave's family had been a part of that congregation for nearly 130 years. There was a sizable endowment that remained, but the congregation was shrinking and getting older. Sadly, the new young pastor who came several years earlier didn't respect the congregants or their spiritual journeys, referring to them in the end as "cultural Christians." He had a vision to close the church and use the endowment to begin a storefront church in the middle of the downtown area, something completely alien to the current membership. That was a vision that never materialized. There were resources, and there was life left in that congregation. Certainly, the "good old days" loomed large in the memories of those who remained, but the lack of leadership was staggering, and it led to tremendous grief, guilt, and anger.

To use Robert Quinn's framework, congregations like Dave's childhood parish are in the process of slow death. But the important thing to remember about congregations in the process of slow death is that they are not dead yet. *They are not dead yet!* They can still touch the lives of many and still provide faithful ministry. They can still be part of what God is up to in the world. They can still do all this, even though the experience of the last decades' failed attempts at growth and renewal offer evidence that long-term survival is unlikely. They can do this whether they face the reality of their situation or not because, no matter the circumstances, God is still at work in and through them.

Here are some indicators that suggest a congregation is in the process of slow death:

- An aging membership
- Declining financial resources
- Increasing dependence on endowment to fund current expenses

- Growing reliance on fund-raising ventures to support current expenses
- Repeated failed attempts to attract new members
- Resistance to conversations about the congregation's long-term future
- Ongoing reference to past "glory" days
- Avoidance of conversations about decline
- Persistent talk about the ways God will provide so that the congregation will survive
- Little follow-through on plans for change in its approach to ministry

While one type of remembering congregation may be in decline, like Dave's childhood parish, another might appear quite different. In fact, it may look as though it's thriving. This congregation can maintain both its building and its ministry with little problem. It often relies on a regular stream of new members. In warmer climates, for example, a steady stream of retirees who were active in their northern congregations might provide a continuing flow of new members. Such a congregation may have had to make some adjustments in staffing over the past decade, but it still has a strong sense of vitality. It is often this very vitality that results in remembering being the congregation's formative image, thus making denial likely. On the surface, everything looks great. There is no need to change. What it has been and done in the past it can continue to be and do. What can easily be ignored (or denied) in this scenario is the long-term trends related to membership and finances. Consider again our warm climate congregation example. Although retirees will continue to move to warmer climates, and the rate might even increase, it is quite likely that the number of those who have been active in northern congregations will decrease. The pool of new members will become smaller, and, when it does, decline will become inevitable. It might not look that way at all right now, making it easy to ignore/deny, but decline is a realistic likelihood. As such, congregations, even seemingly thriving ones, would do well to consider their long-term prospects and what they mean for their continuing ministry. The question may be asked, "What is the motivation for a thriving church to look more deeply into its structure and ministry?" Our response is simply this, because God is calling us to be ever vigilant and ever faithful.

As we noted above, denial is a common response to the prospect of slow death. It takes gentle, compassionate leadership to guide a congregation to accept this reality. Some may recognize this, but many will resist it. The responsibility of those who see it is to awaken others in as gentle a way as possible, even as the congregation continues to go about life in as normal a way as possible. It is important to remember that, despite all else, for most congregations important and faithful ministry is still happening. This is what the pastoral leadership in Dave's childhood congregation didn't understand.

While faithful ministry may still be happening, helping a remembering congregation begin to face the reality of possible or likely death can enhance its ministry. An array of obstacles makes this difficult in both a declining and a thriving congregation. These obstacles operate mostly in quite subtle ways. In our experience, three are particularly powerful, so we'll consider three approaches that may help overcome them. You will need to decide which, if any, apply to your setting. The approach we take in all three is based in a belief that self-discovery leads to the deepest learning. In discussing each obstacle we offer experiences with the potential to enable a discussion that will lead people to greater acceptance of the reality they are facing. We will offer brief overviews of each of them first and then add fuller explanations and ideas for discussion. We encourage you to select one that relates to your congregation's experience and use the suggestions we offer.

We have mentioned this before, but we want to repeat it here. As you help members of the congregation face denial, remember two things: 1) they have not failed; important ministry is still happening; and 2) they cannot be forced to give up their denial; they must accept it on their own.

Change means engaging the unknown. Sometimes resistance to doing this comes from a fear of the loss that will happen or a desire to avoid the grief of loss. If that is the case, it is helpful to explore the inevitability of endings occurring regularly in life. As people perceive the endings they face within a larger framework, it can lessen the notion of failure.

In other cases, the obstacle may be difficulty confronting any dimension of the congregation that is not positive and successful. They are proud of the congregation and what it has done and continues to do. For such people, any criticism of the congregation is often difficult to understand and accept. In this case, exploring the great paradox that the church has always been may help people begin to admit the difficult realities that face their congregation. The letters of Paul provide clear evidence of the church as both a source of love, acceptance, and grace, as well as a place of controversy, misunderstanding, and ego rivalry. That paradox continues today.

Finally, there are times in which all of us engage in dysfunctional behaviors because they create a stability or security for our lives and allow us to avoid facing more difficult aspects of life. In his book *Addiction and Grace,* Gerald May, the late psychiatrist and senior fellow at the Shalem Institute, notes that even the best-intentioned of us are caught in patterns of addiction we don't recognize and accept; it is the human condition.[1] All humans, he believes, yearn for a deep and intimate relationship with God. And yet we also fear what might be asked of us in that relationship. Addictive behaviors are avoidance mechanisms we adopt to escape this dilemma. These behaviors may be the way some have chosen to avoid the difficulty of facing the possibility of impending death. Let's explore these three obstacles now in more depth.

ENDINGS

The need to face endings can be seen in three different scenarios. First, in some congregations, resistance to the elimination of programming or to the consideration of closing the congregation is based on a fear that they will be seen as failing. When Dave interviewed several members of his childhood parish after it had closed, he found a profound sense among them that they had failed, and it was devastating to them. When this is the case, a congregation can benefit from reflection on endings as a natural part of life.

Secondly, while not in danger of closing, many congregations expend untold amounts of energy maintaining programs and activities that out-lived their usefulness years ago. It is not at all unusual to find:

- congregations that have a Christmas Fair because they have always had a Christmas Fair, even though it taxes the energy and patience of everyone involved and no longer provides support for the congregation's budget as it once did;
- congregations that maintain a cumbersome board structure because that's the way they have always done it or because it is what the denomination says is needed, even though there are no longer enough people who are able and willing to serve;
- congregations that simply let old programs quietly fade away when no one participates any longer because to acknowledge their demise would be seen as admitting failure;
- congregations that continue to try one congregational renewal strategy after another even though none of them has produced results.

Thirdly, the need for ending features of congregational life is true in a broader sense as well. Phyllis Tickle, in her book *The Great Emergence*, discussed four great transition points for the church.[2] These are the first three:

- In the fifth and sixth century the development of monasteries provided a new expression for the church at the time of the fall of the Roman Empire, to which it had been closely linked.
- In the eleventh century the church split into eastern and western branches with differing understandings of faith and practice.
- In the sixteenth century profound change came to the church through the Protestant Reformation and the Catholic Counter-Reformation.

Each of these, she said, required the church to conduct a rummage sale in which old ways of being and doing were let go. This meant the end of practices and beliefs that had been assumed as central, but it was a way for the church to reform itself in a changing world. As she looked at the state of the church today, she believed that we are in yet another great transition.

If the church is to move into the future, it first needs to let go of the past, which means it needs to end things, even things that have been important. But there is much at work in most people that leads us to resist facing the loss of something that is important to us. In *Necessary Endings* clinical psychologist and leadership coach Henry Cloud discusses reasons people resist facing the reality of necessary endings. He believes it is essential to overcome this resistance: "Endings are not only part of life; they are a requirement for living and thriving, professionally and personally. Being alive requires that we sometimes kill off things in which we were once invested, uproot what we previously nurtured, and tear down what we built for an earlier time."[3] If you sense that this resistance may be at work in your situation, but people are able to consider the impact of these factors in their own lives, here is one way to initiate reflection and conversation.

- Provide each person with a copy of the Endings Worksheet (on the last page of this chapter).

- Explain that its main purpose is to provide a way of personal reflection on factors that may be at work in our lives as we face the need for change. You might say something like this: "Change is difficult, and it is natural to resist coming to terms with the need for it. Since we all face multiple changes in our lives, we create patterns of behavior that help us deal with them. This can be helpful in that it provides time for us to come to terms with the reality of the need for change. But it can also be problematic if it causes us to resist facing the change that is needed or inevitable. Either way, it is good to be aware of what is at work in us as we face change. That is what this worksheet helps us do."

- Assure them that this is personal work, and that they will not be asked to share anything with the group that they do not want to share.

- Point out the rating scale to be used: 0 for not a factor for me to 5 for a very powerful factor for me.

- Check to see if there are any questions about the purpose or the process.

- Allow ten to fifteen minutes for personal work.

- When you bring the group back together, remind them that they do not need to share anything they do not want to share, but that if there is something they'd like to offer, they are welcome to do so. After they have shared, ask an open-ended question about the experience, such as "What was doing this like for you?" or "Did you learn anything new about yourself?"

This worksheet and the discussion are intended to help people do the "personal gut check" that is the first step in overcoming resistance to change. If you believe the group members are open to a discussion of endings related to the congregation, you might ask something such as, "Do any of you sense that the concerns we've mentioned are at play in discussions about the future of our church?"

There is also a corporate dimension to overcoming a resistance to facing the need for endings. How has the congregation handled ending programs or traditions in the past? What are the customary ways it responds to the possibility of endings? The following questions provide a beginning point for a discussion of issues related to endings from a corporate perspective. They are grouped according to particular issues. Select the issue that is most pertinent to your congregation. Then use the questions as a guide for group discussion. Here's a way you might do that:

- Review the list of issues and select one that addresses a concern that is present in the congregation and offers the best possibility of a fruitful discussion.

- Introduce the group to the notion that congregations, like all organizations, have established ways of dealing with issues in their corporate life. One of those issues is the way in which the organization faces and deals with the need to change by discontinuing existing programs and practices.

- If you believe the group will be open to this, you might reflect on something that has happened in the congregation that illustrates this point.

- Explain the area that you have selected to discuss and offer the suggested question(s) or ones that you think will work better at encouraging discussion.

- As the discussion develops, periodically share what you see as the main points.

- As the discussion concludes, ask if it has provided any insight into ways in which the congregation can better address issues related to endings.

Here is a list of the issues and their related questions:

1. Questions to help see endings as a normal part of life instead of as a problem or a failure.

    - What was the reaction when a decision was made to end programs or traditions of the congregation in the past?
    - How has the congregation responded when a pastor resigned?
    - Does the congregation begin and end programs on a regular basis? What are the reasons for the beginning or the ending?

2. Questions to determine if there is an overload of programming.

    - To what extent does offering the activities and programs the church provides require significant effort of those involved?

- Do leaders in the church talk about how much work there is to do or how few people there are to help?
- If people are reluctant to serve on boards and committees, what reasons do they give?

3. Questions to consider possible barriers to accepting endings.

- Are any of the following present in the congregation? If so, to what extent?
- Is there a desire to avoid making others look bad?
- Is there a feeling that ending something means we have failed?
- Is there a loyalty to a person, the past, or a tradition that makes it difficult to end something?

4. Questions to help accept the difficult reality that more effort won't change things.

- Is there a current program or effort in the congregation that hasn't worked the way you hoped it would, even though you have kept trying to succeed?
- What is keeping you involved?
- What would it take to admit that more effort won't change things?

5. Questions to help determine what is genuine hope and what is just wishful thinking.

- Have there been times in the congregation's life when it was discovered that what was thought of as being hopeful turned out to be just wishful thinking?
- What brought about the change of mind?

6. Questions to help embrace grief.

- How has the congregation handled the conclusion of pro-grams or traditions in the past?
- Would it cause grief for the congregation if some current programs or traditions were discontinued?
- Do all of these programs or traditions continue to be effective and meaningful? If not, what might be involved in letting them go?

7. Questions to help celebrate the new possibilities that can emerge.

- Are there new possibilities for ministry in which the church could engage, but no time to develop them because of the time spent on ministries that may have outlived their usefulness?
- What would these new ministries provide for the community and the congregation?

We need to be clear that, although engaging the material on these worksheets can be a helpful process, it is not an easy one. Resistance can be so great that it may seem impossible to break through. One pastor described the situation this way: "We have gone back to just one worship service since the pandemic. The older parishioners are grieving the loss of their 'traditional' service. I have held that grief, offered a service to let go of things we miss, etc. and instead of them talking to me about it, parking lot conversations are happening. They (maybe a dozen) want church the way it was thirty, forty, fifty years ago. I don't know how to engage them and help them see the need for death there and for change to take root."

PARADOX
From its very beginning the church has been a paradox, weaving together the profound and the pedantic, grace and greed, piety and prejudice. This truth is not easy to face, for it demonstrates how Christians, how the

church, how we are so often far less than we claim to be or wish to be. But to deny this makes dealing with reality all but impossible. There are times when this resistance makes it difficult for a congregation to face the less-positive side of its paradoxical nature. To move beyond this denial, it is helpful to face the paradox head-on and to realize that it is not unique to us but has been true for the church from the very beginning. This is the paradox that is the church:

There are countless people throughout the world whose lives are more meaningful, fulfilling, and fruitful because they are a part of a congregation. There are countless people throughout the world who are no longer hungry or homeless or oppressed or caught in a life of addiction to drugs and alcohol because of the ministries of the church. There are countless people throughout the world who know love and are loving, who know acceptance and are accepting, because they are involved in a congregation. No critique of the church, no engagement with the paradox that is the church can change that. It is true and it is to be celebrated!

But congregations often fail to live up to all they are called (and often claim) to be. When Robert's Rules of Order takes on more importance than discerning the will of God when making decisions. When determining the color of the sanctuary carpet results in a battle of wills. When ministry is reduced to a plethora of programming that burns leaders out. When a sense of entitlement on the part of big givers and longtime members thwarts faithfulness in ministry. When the blame game can too easily be played and the things I want become more important than faithfully serving God or when power takes precedence over prayer.

There is no way to avoid it, the church in all its expressions (local, regional, and national) is a great paradox. It is at one and the same time a holy community that manifests the love of God and a dysfunctional organization that frustrates, angers, exhausts, and sometimes consumes those who participate in it. When the fullness of the paradox is not faced, the church easily becomes a fantasyland of pious pretensions and deceitful dreams, unable to be honest with itself and others.

Paul saw a similar paradox in the church at Corinth. He attempted to deal with it in his first letter to them, as he confronts the issue of conflict in the church.

> Now I appeal to you, brothers and sisters, by the name of our Lord Jesus Christ, that all of you be in agreement and that there be no divisions among you, but that you be united in the same mind and the same purpose. For it has been reported to me by Chloe's people that there are quarrels among you, my brothers and sisters. What I mean is that each of you says, "I belong to Paul," or "I belong to Apollos," or "I belong to Cephas," or "I belong to Christ." Has Christ been divided? Was Paul crucified for you? Or were you baptized in the name of Paul? I thank God that I baptized none of you except Crispus and Gaius, so that no one can say that you were baptized in my name. (I did baptize also the household of Stephanas; beyond that, I do not know whether I baptized anyone else.) For Christ did not send me to baptize but to proclaim the gospel, and not with eloquent wisdom, so that the cross of Christ might not be emptied of its power. (1 Corinthians 1:10–17)

Here are some questions that can be used in a discussion of this passage:

- What do you think is the problem Paul is attempting to address?
- What is your reaction to the presence of controversy even this early in the church?
- Why do you think that conflict developed?
- In what ways does this resonate with the experience in your congregation?

Here are some questions for a general discussion:

- What do you cherish most about our congregation?
- In what way would you like it to grow as a community of faith?
- How well do you think we handle differences?
- As you look to the future, what do you hear God calling our congregation to do or be?

Here are some questions based on the content that is presented:

- Share the above indented paragraphs that talk about the paradox of the church, introducing it by saying "it is one person's perspective that they may not agree with."
- Do you think this is an accurate picture of the church in general? Our congregation?
- In what ways is our congregation like this description? In what ways is it different?
- If the church is really as paradoxical as this, how do you handle it? Do you ignore the less-positive things? Are you frustrated by them? Do you cope with them as best you can? Do you just focus on the positive things?

ADDICTION

As we mentioned above, Gerald May notes addictive behaviors are often used to avoid facing realities we would rather not face. In this case, it may be the difficult possibility that God is asking the congregation to die to make resurrection possible. These avoidance mechanisms are not necessarily overtly destructive, but they can all keep us from engaging more deeply with God.

Addiction isn't just personal, however. It also has a corporate form. Richard Rohr's book *Breathing Underwater: Spirituality and the Twelve Steps* is primarily about personal addiction. But, as he notes in the introduction, "Our inability to see our personal failures is paralleled by our inability to see our institutional and national sins too. It is the identical and same pattern of addiction and denial."[4]

In many ways we might well be like the rich young man that Jesus encountered.

> As he was setting out on a journey, a man ran up and knelt before him, and asked him, "Good Teacher, what must I do to inherit eternal life?" Jesus said to him, "Why do you call me good? No one is good but God alone. You know the commandments: 'You shall not murder; You shall not commit adultery; You shall not steal; You shall not bear false witness; You shall not defraud; Honor your father and mother.'" He said to him, "Teacher, I have kept all these since my youth." Jesus, looking at him, loved him and said, "You lack one thing; go, sell what you own, and give the money to the poor, and you will have treasure in heaven; then come, follow me." When he heard this, he was shocked and went away grieving, for he had many possessions. (Mark 10:17–22)

Like the rich young man, we seek a deeper relationship with God and have been earnest in our attempt to do what is needed for that. Also like him we are attached to things that bring us status, security, and a way of life and faith we find comfortable. Perhaps we also fear that God will ask us, as Jesus asked the young man, to give up those things to grow more deeply in relationship with God. We fail to see, as did the young man, that these are addictions and that they play the same role in our lives that they did in his. And so, we avoid that deeper encounter. All of this can be true for individual Christians, but it can also be true for a congregation. It, too, can occupy itself with countless activities that are in fact addictions. These keep the congregation from a deeper involvement with God and God's work in the world because it is afraid of what God might ask of it and what might be lost.

Reflection on this passage can be a helpful way to introduce the notion of addiction. After sharing the passage with the group, select some of these questions for discussion:

- What do you think motivated the rich man's question? Do you think it was sincere, that he was seeking to find a way to be more faithful?

- Why does he resist Jesus's response?

- One possible way to look at this passage is to see a tension within the man—on the one hand wanting to deepen his faith and on the other hand being afraid to give up his possessions to do that. In that sense the possessions are an addiction that keeps him from the deeper faith he seeks. Do you experience a similar tension in your own desire to grow in faith?

- What might have helped the man take the risk of following Jesus?

Church-related religious activities are among the most compelling of these addictions because they give the appearance of being about faith. They permit us to feel close to God while still being in control and not actually engaging God at a deep level. Our inability to recognize these behaviors for what they are and wean ourselves from them leads inevitably to an increasing separation from God, which results in dysfunction and a decline in our ability to be the congregation God has called us to be.

So what are these addictive behaviors that keep us from facing the hard realities of decline and eventual death that may well be God's way of calling us to a new way of church? They can be just about anything. The key is that they have become the focus of our involvement, the things we are attached to and not willing to let go of. We hang on to our addictions to protect ourselves from whatever it is we fear. We can begin to discover them by considering the things we believe are most important to our experience of church. It might be the liturgy, the role of the clergy, the sense of family, the style of music, the order of worship, the polity, a particular social issue, the mission and outreach we are engaged in. But they might also be less overtly religious, such as the sense of authority we achieve from leadership in the congregation, the friends we value, the sense of fulfillment we get from helping others, the assurance that this is the place where our funeral will occur. It's not that any of these is inherently wrong, only that when they become what is most important to us they become obstacles keeping us from God; they become addictions or, in the language of faith, they become idols. When we are unable to face life without them, we are also unable to face the reality of the institution that provides them for us no longer existing. It becomes impossible to consider the prospect of slow death.

This idolatry is what lies at the root of Jesus's criticism of the religious elite of his day. In their straining gnats and swallowing camels (Matthew 23:24) and other practices, they had developed attachments that kept them and others from experiencing the love of God more fully and sharing that love.

This is also the dynamic Paul challenged in his letter to the Galatians, who had focused their religious life around a specific ritual, circumcision: "For freedom Christ has set us free; stand fast therefore, and do not submit again to a yoke of slavery" (Galatians 5:1). The ritual had become an addiction that was an obstacle to knowing God more fully. It had entrapped them, so they were no longer free to relate fully to God and each other.

One of the reasons addictions are so difficult to overcome is that we are often unaware of them, and when they do begin to become apparent, we deny or hide them. Rohr explains this situation well: "There are shared and agreed-upon addictions in every culture and institution. These are often the hardest to heal because they do not look like addictions because we have all agreed to be compulsive about the same things and blind to the same problems."[5] When blindness is no longer possible, denial, which is the defense system of all addicts, sets in.

When congregations first face the reality of declining membership and finances, the typical response is to seek a quick fix that will correct the situation. So they busy themselves with strategies intended to reverse the decline: creating new programs, hosting more social events, beginning a strategic planning process, restructuring or rewriting the bylaws. The possibilities are all but endless, but each of them is little more than another avoidance mechanism eagerly adopted to circumvent engaging in the difficult, and often painful, work of looking deeply to discover the patterns and consequences of addictive behavior and how it blocks the ability to deal with real concerns. On it goes, until at some point the pain of avoidance becomes greater than the fear they have been seeking to avoid.

When this happens, a congregation will struggle and suffer, blaming and conflict will become commonplace. But it is also a time when hope can begin to emerge. For amid suffering, it is possible that a new awareness will arise—an awareness that something else is needed, that whatever efforts have been made to make things better simply have not worked. This is the time, as it is with all addicts, that the possibility of truly, deeply, honestly turning to God emerges. For congregations it is a time when the reality of being caught in a process of slow death can be faced.

The twelve-step program of Alcoholics Anonymous is undoubtedly the most well-known and widespread approach to addressing personal addictive behavior. Many see it as a practical spirituality because it calls upon addicts to look deeply into their own lives, acknowledge the need for a power greater than themselves, and make the changes that are necessary for well-being. We believe it can provide helpful insights for congregations in facing their own addictive behaviors. This doesn't mean that the meeting of the governing board should be used as an intervention, but we do believe there are important insights to be gained from twelve-step programs that can help a congregation move beyond its addictions so that it can recognize and accept the slow death that is occurring. It encourages the congregation to face its powerlessness to overcome its addictions on its own. It asks the people, with that knowledge, to recognize that a power beyond themselves is needed and to turn the congregation over to that power. This enables them to face themselves and the situation of their congregation honestly. It then becomes possible to turn those issues over to the higher power and ask that they be removed. With this change, a congregation can face the harm it has caused to others and seek to make amends. Members of the congregation are urged to continue their communal inventory, deepen their relationship with God, and continue to practice the principles they have developed during the process.

The movement in this process is one toward greater honesty with self and others, facing the reality of the congregation's situation, and doing those things that will enable them to move beyond their previous addictive pattern of life. This can be a helpful process for those congregations that have been unable to face the reality of slow death. It encourages greater honesty, greater reliance on God, and movement out of the patterns of thought and behavior that resulted in denial.

While the process can be helpful to congregations, it will need to be approached in a very different way than it is with individuals. We don't envision great success coming from a declaration that the members of the congregation are a bunch of addicts! Once again, an approach more likely to lead to deeper awareness is one based in asking questions. Here are some possible discernment questions, loosely modeled on AA's twelve steps, that might help a congregation begin to look more deeply and honestly at the reality of avoidance:

- Have our efforts to address concerns related to membership, financial decline, and other issues related to the future viability of the congregation produced the results for which we hoped?

- Is it likely that continuing these efforts will produce the results we seek?

- In what ways have we sought God's will for our congregation?

- What assumptions, hopes, and fears might be blocking our willingness to be open to God's leading?

- How can we be more forthright with ourselves and God about our inability to address the issues that concern us?

- In what ways can we share with God and others our failure to set aside our personal desires in making decisions about the future of the congregation?

- Are we ready to let go of our personal hopes for the future of the congregation and be open to God's call to us?

- Are there old ways we need to let go of? How do we do that?

- In what ways have we avoided facing realities about the future because we fear what our conclusions might be?

- How can we look honestly at the reality of our future and make decisions based on that?

- In what ways can we continue to explore our future as a congregation with a focus on discerning God's will for us?

- How do we discern ways in which we can share God's love more fully in our congregation and community?

- How can we continue to open ourselves more fully to ways in which we can share God's love with others?

The notion of addictive behavior impacting the life of a congregation may be new to many and might be difficult for them to accept, especially if it involves looking at the congregation's own addictive behavior. Hopefully the discernment questions we have offered provide a gentle way into a discussion that will lead to a realization of the role addictive behavior plays in preventing a congregation from facing the reality of the slow death it may be experiencing. It is hard work, no doubt, but we believe that it is essential if congregations are to face the reality of their current situations and open themselves to God's leading.

The suggestions we have offered in this chapter can be used to help a congregation move beyond denial and accept its impending or eventual closure. We encourage you to consider and develop other ways in which you may do this. It is important to recognize, however, that even if you have not enabled denial and have provided opportunities for the congregation to move beyond the obstacles to facing reality, it may be that a congregation will not accept the reality of eventual death until it is time to close the doors. Even if that is the case, the congregation can still have a significant ministry, acting faithfully to do the right thing in its time and place. It may provide the continuing nurture and support needed to sustain the life and faith of those for whom traditional ways are essential. It may provide a safe place to find comfort in the midst of the turmoil of a changing world. It may provide a community of acceptance and friendship. It may even provide a place of denial for those who do not yet have the resources to face the reality that lies before them. God will continue to be at work, even if the denial persists.

ENDINGS WORKSHEET

Change (which always means letting go of the present and things that are important to us) is difficult. When faced with this prospect it is not unusual to resist the reality that we face. This is human nature, a trait all of us have in common. Below is a list of attitudes and behaviors that underlie that resistance. Read over this list. Consider your own response to changes you have experienced and the need to end things that have been important to you. Then rate each item 0 to 5 according to how true it is for you. Mark 0 for not at all through 5 for very much. Although we will have a general discussion of this experience, you will not need to share specific ratings.

_____ I am afraid people will think I'm giving up.

_____ I continue to think the problem can be fixed.

_____ I don't want to upset others.

_____ I am afraid people will think my faith is not strong.

_____ I don't want to take responsibility for ending something that has been important to me and others.

_____ I don't know how to do it.

_____ I don't know how to explain it to others so that they will understand.

_____ I am afraid of the void that will be left.

_____ I don't know how to handle the grief that might come with the loss.

_____ I don't want to deal with how I might be perceived by others.

NOTES

1. Gerald May, *Addiction and Grace: Love and Spirituality in the Healing of Addictions* (New York: HarperOne, 1988), xi.

2. Phyllis Tickle, *The Great Emergence: How Christianity Is Changing and Why* (Grand Rapids: Baker, 2008), 19–31.

3. Henry Cloud, *Necessary Endings* (New York: HarperCollins, 2010), 8.

4. Richard Rohr, *Breathing Underwater: Spirituality and the Twelve Steps* (Cincinnati: Franciscan Media, 2011), xxii.

5. Rohr, xxiii.

CHAPTER 4

Letting Go

Insights from Hospice

Very truly, I tell you,
unless a grain of wheat falls into the earth and dies,
it remains just a single grain;
but if it dies, it bears much fruit.

—JOHN 12:24

IF A CONGREGATION CAN RECOGNIZE THE REALITY OF DECLINE, ACCEPT that there is little chance of reversing that trend, and admit the probability of its death, new possibilities arise. Even if the death is years away, facing its likelihood can be an important step, because it can lead to a reorientation of both thinking and action, as well as provide new insights for ministry.

Death is never easy. The death of a congregation that has been a meaningful part of our lives is something none of us want to face. Sometimes a congregation is forced to let go of aspects of its life and ministry because there is no alternative—the person who held a program together died or moved away, money to fund the staff position could no longer be covered in the budget. At other times a congregation can make decisions about what to let go of—a Bible study that was once highly popular now has only a few participants, the Christmas bazaar that once contributed significant funds to the church's mission effort no longer attracts the numbers of people that made that possible.

Whatever the reason, significant changes are difficult to face. The dying that is involved in these experiences brings with it a great sense of loss and failure—perhaps even a feeling of being abandoned by God. But if we accept this difficult reality and respond with an openness to the Spirit's leading, it can become possible to let go of what has been.

Henri Nouwen, in *Our Greatest Gift*, writes that dying well is one of the best gifts we can give to others. We believe this insight applies not only to human beings but to faith communities as well. Dying well becomes a greater possibility for congregations whose formative image is letting go than for those whose formative image is remembering.

These congregations, like remembering congregations, are in a process of slow death. They differ in that they have overcome the obstacles to facing that reality and no longer exist in denial. This, undoubtedly, required a significant effort on their part. They have had to realize that the decline that has taken place in previous years will likely not be reversed. They have had to curtail programs and traditions that they have cherished in the past. They have had to grieve their losses. If they have done this, then they are able to consider what the coming days of the congregation will be. Once they have accepted the reality of slow death, they can begin to consider the way in which they will die. That provides new opportunities for the congregation's life and ministry. In considering what it will be about, the congregation can learn from an organization that focuses on encountering death in a positive way—hospice.

Jeff remembers: "Early in my ministry I explained to a parishioner that a church member who had been ill for a long time was entering hospice care. Her response was to ask, 'Is she giving up?' I replied, 'No, she is letting go.'" Letting go of the struggle and the pain, letting go of the endless striving. Letting go and simply falling into the hands of God. Thankfully, in the years since, personal hospice care has for many people come to be seen as more than simply giving up. Unfortunately, this has not happened in the discussion of what hospice care might look like for congregations. Talking about hospice care for a congregation isn't widely done, and when it is, people of faith often reject it. It is seen as negative and defeatist, as losing hope, as lacking faith in the power of God. But there is another way to look at it. The insights that come from hospice offer a faithful and hopeful perspective for congregations that are letting go of what they have been but are still providing significant opportunities for people to minister faithfully in many ways.

One way to look at the purpose of personal hospice care is to see it as the bringing together of resources to maintain the highest possible quality of life for a person who has accepted the reality of his or her impending death. This can also inspire great hope for congregations that wish to consider the ways in which dying might be a part of living into the future. While this may be difficult, there is no need to be fatalistic about the thought of dying. It isn't an admission of failure or of giving up. It is a means of looking to the future in both a realistic and hopeful way.

We believe that the hospice metaphor provides helpful insights. Hospice care for a congregation is not giving up but letting go—resting in the hands of God while seeking a high quality of life and ministry in whatever time remains. It addresses the actual death of the congregation itself and the death of old ways of being a congregation. For this to happen, however, the congregation must first be willing to consider the reality of the death it faces. Personal hospice care cannot be effective if the people involved want to continue seeking a cure or maintaining life as long as possible. There needs to be a change in their thinking, a change of heart, that brings a shift in what they do. In personal hospice care this is a decision to move away from a curative position to a palliative one. The treatments and procedures that are used when seeking a cure are set aside and the focus becomes the treatments and procedures that will enhance the person's quality of comfort and well-being even as the process of dying continues. Since these approaches are usually mutually exclusive, it is necessary to choose one or the other.

Similarly, congregations cannot continue to long for a return to the good old days or the revitalization of old programs and ways. They cannot continue to hold on to a false hope of renewal and focus their efforts on strategies intended to increase membership and financial resources. These are all "curative" strategies. Instead, it is essential to face the likelihood, if not the inevitability, of death and begin to adopt "palliative" strategies.

When this change in orientation takes place, a new way of being and doing becomes possible. These congregations will continue to do all they can do for as long as they can do it. Pastoral care will be given. Spiritual growth will be encouraged. Mission to the community will continue. Worship will remain central to its life. The fellowship of the community will continue to be experienced. All of these ministries will occur, not in the belief that they will bring new members or renewal of programs but rather because these are the things that enhance the quality of life of a congregation; these are the things congregations do as they share God's love with each other and the world.

But there will eventually be a letting go—perhaps of the full-time pastor, of the building, of the traditional organizational structure, of the prominent position in the community, of significant and meaningful traditions. In some cases, this letting go may lead the congregation into a new way of being church. In other cases, it will lead to a decision to disband. In either case there will, of course, be much to grieve. There will also still be much to cherish and much love to share. But first facing the reality and likelihood of death is necessary. Without that, efforts will still be focused on growth strategies, hopes will still be held out for a return to the way things used to be. Without that, it will be impossible to cherish while letting go and celebrate while grieving. By facing the reality and likelihood of death, there is a real possibility of making meaningful end-of-life decisions—priorities to set for the remaining time, provisions to make for the time when death comes and the legacy that will be left behind.

While we considered the reality of denial in the previous chapter, it is such a significant force that it will be wise to remind ourselves using insights from the experience of hospice. Often, even in a congregation that has brought itself to face the reality of death, there will be those for whom the thought of hospice care might well be abhorrent. Denial exercises a powerful pull on those who are facing painful realities, and some are just not able to overcome that pull. Personal hospice care recognizes the important function denial plays for those who are not yet ready to deal with the issues surrounding death. In her book *Final Journeys: A Practical Guide for Bringing Care and Comfort at the End of Life,*

Maggie Callanan, a nurse focusing on care of the dying, explains this well: "Denial is a powerful crutch that should not be yanked away unless you have something more powerful and supportive to put in its place. . . . Denial will be given up if and when the patient (or family member) is able to deal with the truth. On rare occasions it is never given up. If that happens, so be it."[1] This is true for congregations, too. It is not wise to confront denial directly if the "something more powerful and supportive" that Callahan talks about isn't available. It is important, however, not to support expressions of denial. What is possible is to attempt to lead the resistant members of the congregation to a greater awareness of their situation in a way that will enable them to overcome their need for denial.

Congregations that are considering the need to curtail traditional and meaningful programs or to make major adjustments in their ways (such as a reduced staff or a part-time pastor) may also find it difficult to accept the death involved in these changes. They all involve significant loss that should be recognized and grieved. Even in the midst of the grief, the congregation can celebrate for the role these past experiences played in its life and ministry.

Facing the impending closure of a congregation or the elimination of meaningful aspects of what has been can be a significant challenge. It requires sensitivity, strength, and courage to lead a people into a willingness to accept hospice care. It also requires a personal grounding that allows leaders to receive the anger that will inevitably be directed toward them without taking it personally and reacting to it. For many congregations today, however, death is a real possibility that needs to be engaged. When this reality becomes clear, the process of dying will still be difficult and filled with grief. However, there is also a real possibility that death will lead to resurrection.

As the congregation accepts the reality of the death it is facing, it becomes possible to be more forthright about the insights that come from hospice. Here are several that will be important to keep in mind and discuss. Not all will speak to your situation, so choose those that do. We suggest that you share the description and then ask group members to respond to it before asking them to articulate the ways they think it might apply to your congregation. Depending on the participants, it might be helpful to begin the discussion by asking them to share their own experience with hospice. This may elicit strong emotions, but it can also provide a foundation for considering the possibility of hospice care related to the life of the congregation. Obviously, this will require a sensitivity to all those involved and an awareness of their experiences.

Here are the insights that we believe can be helpful to a congregation: *Sooner rather than later.* It is important to let people make the decision about hospice care on their own, when they are ready to let go of the helpful crutch that denial provides. That being said, it's also important to realize that it is better to make this decision sooner rather than later, especially to avoid delaying it until a point in time near the end of the congregation's viable existence. Maggie Callanan puts it this way as she talks about personal hospice care: "Hospice is remarkable in what it can do to help patients and their families cope with an illness that cannot be cured. What it can do is very impressive, *but only if the hospice staff are given enough time to do it.*"[2] The same is true for hospice care for a congregation in the process of slow death. With time, attention can be given to an array of important concerns from grieving together, to discerning a legacy, to conserving resources to underwrite that legacy. But all of this takes time, hence, the reason to move to a hospice mindset as soon as possible.

The transition from curative to palliative care. We talked about this earlier in the chapter, but it bears repeating because it is undoubtedly the most important insight that hospice care brings to a congregation. It will be an issue that reemerges on a consistent basis. The parallel to the curative care of individuals for a congregation would be any strategy that has the intention of attracting new members, raising additional funds, and restoring the congregation to the promise of what it once was. If these motivated the congregation in the past, force of habit might be all that is needed for them to reemerge even after the congregation has determined that such strategies will not be effective in its current context. They are also likely to reemerge if just one new family becomes involved, which can raise hopes of a growth spurt that might enable the congregation to thrive once again. Palliative care for the congregation means doing those things that the congregation has traditionally been involved with that contribute to a positive sense of well-being. Examples we mentioned earlier are pastoral care, spiritual growth, mission involvement, worship, and fellowship. In many ways a focus on palliative care frees a congregation simply to be the church as it lets go of survival, maintenance, and growth concerns. The various elements of palliative care will continue as long as resources are available and they contribute positively to the congregation's experience. When they no longer do that, it will be time to let them go.

A mix of inward and outward focus. The dying person needs time to reflect, to come to terms with what is happening, and to rest. It is also important, however, that he or she engages others, maintaining relationships with family and friends to keep regular patterns alive as much as possible while receiving the support that is needed from others. The specific mix of these two involvements will vary from person to person, but some form of the mix is important. The same is true for congregations. It is important for them to make time to be inwardly focused, to be together, to process all that is happening to them, and to consider how best to move forward. But this need not be to the exclusion of an outward focus. They are still a congregation that has a mission. They still have resources to devote to that mission. Maintaining the balance of an inward focus and an outward one is essential.

The rejection of life-prolonging strategies. A person in hospice care forgoes treatments that are intended solely to prolong life. This involves making some very difficult decisions, such as discontinuing feeding and having a Do Not Resuscitate order. For a congregation it will mean avoiding engaging in attempts to "fix" their decline or to use their resources in ways that might keep things going a few months or a year longer but have no lasting impact on the process of slow death. It might be difficult to resist a grant or to refuse to use endowment funds to underwrite the cost of a consultant who promises great things, but that is what is needed.

The use of limited resources. There are limits to the resources that are available to a person in hospice care. For most people, there are limited financial resources. For everyone, there are energy and time limitations. A congregation faces limitations as well. For many, financial resources are already dwindling. There are also limits to the energy of those who have worked so hard to sustain the congregation for so long. These limited resources are a major factor in deciding not to employ life-prolonging strategies for both a person and a congregation. The issue for both is how best to use the remaining resources available to them to enhance the experience of those involved.

The importance of grieving. Grieving is essential, because it helps us confront the reality of our own impending death or the death of someone we love. Without acknowledging grief, the immediate experience becomes even more painful, even when that pain is hidden or denied, and the future becomes even more difficult. Once again, this insight from personal hospice care can offer a helpful perspective for congregations. It is essential to recognize, affirm, and celebrate the role any congregation facing death has played in the lives of people. It is a place of community; it has provided support in difficult times and people to celebrate with in joyful times; it may well have been the place of baptisms, confirmations, weddings, and funerals that served as cherished markers in life. It is not easy to let go of all of that. Of course, it is painful, and there is a need to grieve.

Memory making. In reflecting on the choices a person in hospice care must make, Maggie Callanan writes: "To die is a given; but there are still choices to be made. You can spend your remaining time raging against the injustice of it all, or you can acknowledge the inevitable, mourn it, and then get down to the business of memory making. It's a difficult choice, but it's yours to make."[3] For a congregation, a focus on memory making can mean reflecting on past times, accomplishments, and people who may no longer be remembered regularly but might be recalled by those who were involved. Reflection on the past can lead to remembering times of support and encouragement as the congregation or its members faced hardship and difficulty. Remembering these times can bring a new perspective to the ways this support continues and is vital for the current situation. It can bring meaning from the past to provide meaning for the present. More importantly, it might provide the foundation for creating new memories. Memory making can often be enhanced by directing remaining resources toward these activities. It might well be that congregations could direct even their limited resources toward memory making, using them in ways they may not have considered if the priority was prolonging its existence.

Providing a legacy. One of the concerns of most dying people is what they will leave behind—what their legacy will be. This might be financial, but it might also be a way of living or a way of dying. Whatever it is it will be something important to the person that they want others to experience and remember. Congregations have the same opportunity to provide a legacy. This is one of the benefits of accepting the need for hospice care. It offers the chance to consider what the congregation's legacy might be and how to provide it. Some provide for the transfer of remaining funds or the building to others. Others offer memories of their commitment to mission. The possibilities all depend upon those who participate in the life of the congregation, what is important to them, and what they want to provide for the future. The greatest sense of providing a legacy, however, comes when a congregation develops a long-range perspective on the evolution of the church. That is, when it begins to see itself as the seed that produces abundantly only because it is willing to die. As old forms of church die, new ones arise that are more responsive to contemporary and emerging realities. It is this process—which truly is a process of death and resurrection—that makes real Christ's promise that even the gates of hell will not prevail against the church.

We know, of course, that what we are suggesting is a difficult thing to do. We live with the realization that a great deal of what we have said so far challenges much of the focus of our ministries in past years. If your experience is similar, this book will most likely not be an "easy read." You will be challenged. You will probably get angry. Hopefully, you will also get a sense every now and then that we are onto something, that what we are saying resonates with something you have been thinking or feeling. If that is the case, we encourage you to hang in there. There's no telling what God might be up to!

NOTES

1. Maggie Callanan, *Final Journeys: A Practical Guide for Bringing Care and Comfort to the End of Life* (New York: Bantam, 2009), 28.
2. Callanan, 258.
3. Callanan, 203.

CHAPTER 5

Resurrecting

Spirituality and Ethics Revisited

No one sews a piece of unshrunk cloth on an old cloak,
for the patch pulls away from the cloak, and a worse tear is made.
Neither is new wine put into old wineskins;
otherwise, the skins burst, and the wine is spilled . . .
but new wine is put into fresh wineskins . . .
　　　　　　　　　　　　　　　　—MATTHEW 9:16–17

WE CAN FACE THE REALITY OF DEATH BECAUSE WE HAVE FAITH IN RES-
urrection. That's true for us as individuals, but it is also true for the church
and faith communities. The dying church (and here we are speaking of
the forms that the church universal has taken, not an individual congregation) is always also a resurrecting church in which new forms are
emerging. We do not, we cannot, know what form the fully resurrected
church will take any more than we can know what the resurrected body is
like. We do, however, live into the temporary forms of church that emerge
throughout history. That's what happened during Christendom. The
various forms the church took then were not perfect, but they served the
people of God and God's realm in a significant way. In the fifth and sixth
centuries, for example, the "re-formation" of the church within monasteries and convents enabled the church to survive in a time when the Roman
Empire, upon which the church had depended for cultural and political

support, was deteriorating. This new form was smaller, less influential, and certainly less affluent, but it enabled the church to survive and to rid itself of the accretions of culture other forms of church had adopted.

The challenge for congregations whose formative image is resurrecting is to live into another temporary form of church, one better suited to the people and purpose of God in this time. Like most things that have to do with being faithful, it's not easy. There are undoubtedly many ways to go about doing it; no one way can possibly get it completely right.

In this chapter we intentionally avoid the use of the word congregation to refer to resurrecting forms of church. We'll only use it to refer to existing congregations. We do that because we assume and want to make clear that resurrecting as a formative image leads to a variety of expressions. Some of these expressions might look much like existing congregations, but others will not. Some could be semimonastic communities sharing a rule of life. Others could be faith-based nonprofits responding to community needs as they nurture people in faith. Still others could be online communities that enable sharing and support community involvement. And still others could be something we can't even imagine now. So instead of using the term congregations, we will refer to these emergent resurrecting forms of church as faith communities.

While we considered the need for letting go in the previous chapter, a deeper kind of letting go is needed for a faith community whose formative image is resurrecting. This letting go is not so much about programs and staff but rather about basic elements of church life and practice. Virtually nothing should be off the table, for that is the only way we can be certain that we are not ignoring the Spirit because we want to cling to familiar forms of church out of habit or simply because it is personally meaningful to us. The list of potential discussion items should include those that are most often assumed to be essential. It would include the way in which baptism and the eucharist are practiced, the need for buildings, the role and/or need for ordained clergy, the way in which the community engages cultural and political issues, the use of tools such as strategic planning when considering future possibilities. We mention these as illustrations of the kinds of issues we believe need to be discussed to determine the death that is necessary for resurrection to emerge. As a community openly engages in discussions about these and other issues, new ways of being can emerge—new ways that will lead to the death of old ways but also enable new life.

The questions below offer a takeoff point for discussion. They are intentionally provocative in order to stimulate discussion. Select one or two that you think will encourage meaningful sharing. Add issues and questions of your own, as well.

Baptism. Has the way we practice baptism undercut its meaning? A large percentage of baptisms (or infant dedications in those churches that practice believer's baptism) involve parents who rarely attend worship. Parents are asked to agree to an array of prom- ises that in many cases have not been their practice and will not be kept. Could it be that in many cases baptism has become little more than a pageant, portraying something of great importance but betraying the nature of the sacrament or ordinance itself? Might we need to rethink the practice of baptism and the time and circum- stances in which it can be a valid expression of its true nature? Might a better way to celebrate the birth of a child be a service of affirmation of original blessing in which no questions are asked, no promises made, but God's blessing upon the child is celebrated and an acknowledgment of what that blessing means—a celebration of blessing, not a rite of obligation? If baptism is to continue to be one of the essential marks of the church, what form should it take?

What should determine the validity of the eucharist/communion? Months of virtual worship during the coronavirus pandemic which began in 2020 meant that members of the many traditions that require a priestly blessing could not participate in the eucharist. If this rite is central to the faith and sustenance of believers, is that acceptable? Is it possible for those who are at home to partake in a way that is no less meaningful than those who gather for worship led by a priest? The question applies as well to those traditions in which a priestly blessing is not essential. Absent corporate worship, what is it that makes participation in communion meaningful in a way that enriches faith? Can it happen by just grabbing some bread or crackers and some juice and listening to the pastor say a prayer over a live stream? What assumptions about the eucharist/communion need to be set aside? What might replace them?

Have buildings outlived their usefulness? For many people the word "church" is associated primarily with the building in which a congregation meets. Place is important, of course, but many existing congregations are finding that the cost of upkeep consumes a large percentage of their budgets; for some, maintenance has even become impossible. Many buildings were constructed to accommodate a membership much larger than the current one is or has any reasonable expectation of being again. To cover the costs of maintenance, many congregations have had to become landlords for renters. Even if an endowment can provide the needed maintenance, what are the ethical implications of having a building that exceeds any foreseeable needs and draws money away from responding to the needs of people? The virtual church that the coronavirus pandemic necessitated raised further questions about the viability and need for buildings. Might it be time to rethink the use of physical space? Might it be time to begin making plans for the transfer of items located in the church building (such as columbaria) so if (or when) the building is sold they will be cared for? Might this be a time in which to reclaim community, not building, as the primary understanding of church?

Clergy. Should the role of (and need for) ordained clergy be reconsidered? Has what Alan Roxburgh calls "the clergy industry" produced an elitist class more focused on institutional maintenance and order than openness to the Spirit and faithful living? What are the ethical implications of continuing to train people through a process that creates significant personal debt when there are fewer and fewer congregations that can afford full-time clergy? Is it undercutting a more significant role for laity in their own faith and its practice?

Social Issues. Does the way the church engages with culture need to change? In many situations, there is a close identification of a congregation with a political stance or a set of political issues. Existing congregations often divide along "conservative" and "liberal" lines, not just theologically but politically and/or socially. Different congregations support or condemn abortion, seek to limit or enhance immigration, have differing understandings of racial justice, economic disparity and privilege, LGBTQ+ concerns, and environmental issues. These are all political concerns, but they are gospel issues as well because they are all about how we love our neighbor. Often in a congregation in which people have diverse political opinions on potentially divisive subjects that have profound ethical implications, the issues are avoided in the interest of keeping peace. How is the church to navigate these difficult issues without being partisan? Is there a way for it to avoid these difficulties and still practice the ethic of Jesus?

Strategic Planning. Does a reliance on secular planning strategies, such as strategic planning, undercut an ability to prayerfully discern God's leading? Do these practices result in plans that are more in tune with what people want to do than what God is calling the people to do? What would it mean to forego planning and begin to seek ways of discernment?

THE PARABLE OF THE YEAST

While it is true that no one can know the exact form expressions of the church will take, it is possible to begin to imagine qualities they might have. We believe that a helpful metaphor for the church we might live into comes from the parable of the yeast.

> He told them another parable: "The kingdom of heaven is like yeast that a woman took and mixed in with three measures of flour until all of it was leavened." (Matthew 13:33)

In this chapter, in keeping with Brueggemann's insight, we will play with that metaphor a bit and explore what might be involved in using it to shape a community of faith in this time.

The parable of the yeast is about the reign of God. Like the parable of the sower, it addresses both future eschatological concerns and contemporary realities. The reign of God is both "already" and "not yet." The "already" speaks to the church in today's world. Matthew's gospel was in many ways an instruction book for the church of his day—a guidebook for living as faithful followers of Jesus in a society that was shaped by values, ideals, and power relationships that were radically different from the ones Jesus lived and taught. In this way Matthew's setting was not all that different from the one in which we find ourselves. As such, we have much to learn from the insights of the parable and the entire gospel as we attempt to discern a new reality for the church.

A Tiny Part of the Whole

The most obvious insight the parable provides is that yeast is a tiny part of the whole (a small amount amid three measures of flour—enough for 100 loaves of bread). Could it be the church that is emerging is becoming smaller, much smaller than today's church even in its diminished state? And what if Christians understood this smallness as something not to overcome or as a sign of failure prompting worries about survival or frenzied growth strategies but rather as an affirmation of the church being what the church has always been called to be. In our opinion, from the time of Constantine, the underlying operative image of the church has not been yeast but loaf. Rulers determined the faith tradition for the entire state, and everyone was a part of that church. By decree the church exercised authority over all of society, it was the whole loaf. With the end of the state church in the United States, culture provided the props the church needed to remain influential and powerful, incorporating much if not all of society. When the days of Protestant privilege began to wane, and the church began losing its influence, congregational renewal efforts arose to stem the tide of decline. We believe it is time to put an end to this folly.

The metaphor of yeast suggests a church that is small, perhaps even unnoticeable. It is not to be the predominant and powerful institution the Christendom church has attempted to be or that rulers and politicians wanted it to be. That may be appropriate for other institutions, but not the church. It is to be small. In this smallness, its ornate cathedrals, grand rituals, denominational hierarchies, and the accoutrements of clericalism have little or no place. The church is, to put it clearly, to be that small group of people who share a commitment to following Jesus—to being disciples—who are willing (or at the very least earnestly striving) to order their lives around that commitment. Few want to do this. Few can do this. The demands, responsibilities, and attractions of the world are too consuming, but the purpose of the church is to cultivate and sustain disciples. And the only way to accomplish this is not to worry about size at all.

Big Effects

The smallness of yeast itself also provides an insight. In its smallness, it is not sheltered and inwardly focused, as so many congregations tend to be. It is not seeking, above all else, its own survival, cherishing and protecting the cozy fellowship it provides. The metaphor of yeast suggests something far different. As New Testament scholar Warren Carter reminds us, "Relative to the larger amount of flour, . . . the yeast is only a small quantity. Yet its small presence has big effects. The woman literally 'hides' the leaven in the flour. That which seems to be invisible is in fact mysteriously and inevitably performing its leavening work."[1]

This small community has a great mission. Its participants support and nurture each other as disciples, and as disciples they move into the world to do the leavening work of sharing God's love with others. Theirs is a transforming power. In a world where the gap between the rich and poor continues to deepen and more and more families struggle to make ends meet, where consumerism and materialism are primary motivating forces, where systemic racism pervades every institution and women are consistently marginalized, where anti-Semitism is becoming more prevalent, where members of the LBGTQ+ community all too often experience not just a lack of acceptance but outright and sometimes violent hostility—in a world that is becoming increasingly polarized around all of these issues and many more, there can be no doubt that transformation is essential. To live quietly and comfortably in such a society is to reject the gospel. Like yeast, the faith community is to disrupt and corrupt what is, so that it can be transformed. Joan Chittister in her book *The Time Is Now* says this: "No doubt about it: The purpose of prophecy is to leaven the world, to bring it closer to the Reign of God one small step at a time."[2]

Similarly, Gary Peluso-Verdend, executive director of the Center for Religion in Public Life at Phillips Theological Seminary, writes in his commentary on this passage:

> What if a society resembles the empire of Rome much more closely than it does the empire of heaven, expressing in its policies and budget the values of social inequality and redemptive violence? Helping persons to adjust or be balanced to fit into a sick society is not the work of the gospel. . . . The church's work in every age, more so in some ages and places, than in others, is to form disciples who value the contemporary equivalents of . . . yeast.[3]

The metaphor of yeast when applied to a resurrecting church clearly suggests that it will be a small community that is an agent of transformation in the world. This small community is in many ways similar to the community of disciples Jesus called to be with him. His ministry of teaching and healing to all who came was grounded in a small, alternative community of those who lived on the margins of society because of their commitment to him.

This is the way Warren Carter describes the kind of church Matthew is encouraging through his gospel, an image of the church that is shaped by the metaphor of yeast:

> Members of this group participate daily in city life. They speak its language. They work. They walk its streets. They participate in various social and economic networks in order to survive. They

pay taxes. They experience urban poverty and ethnic tensions. Yet in profoundly significant ways, while participants in their society, they comprise another group, a religious community committed to Jesus and addressed by this gospel which offers a different vision of reality, an ideological perspective which, focused on God's empire, shapes an alternative identity and set of practices and social structures for a voluntary marginal existence.[4]

A Transforming/Corrupting Presence

The metaphor of yeast offers yet another insight for the community that has resurrecting as its formative image. In Jesus's day yeast was seen as a symbol of corruption and impurity, "the agent that bloats and rots corpses and what a woman would clean from her house in preparation for Passover."[5] It was most often used as a symbol for the way immorality pervaded society. Jesus, however, took this understanding and turned it on its head, making it an image of God's transforming work in the world. From Jesus's perspective, yeast was a positive and essential agent; from the world's perspective it was anathema. Similarly, the faith community's transforming work in the world as it attempts to bring the reign of God nearer may from the world's perspective be seen as threatening, even as corrupting. If the faith community is small and works for the corruption/ transformation of the values and ways of the existing society, there is a good chance it will be seen by many as something that is subversive and corrupt, something to be rooted out. If the faith community is a small group of deeply committed people, it will be seen as exclusive and elitist and be denounced for that reason. If it addresses the pressing ethical issues of society, it will be seen as too political.

This possibility becomes even clearer when we consider the broader context of Matthew in which this parable appears. Jesus's ministry was in many ways a bold critique of not only the social and political world in which he lived but also the religious establishment that dominated that world. When Jesus challenged the scribes and Pharisees, he was challenging a religious establishment that had become more concerned about its rules and rituals than faithfulness. He was challenging a hierarchy that was more concerned about its position and privilege than people. He was challenging a religious system that was more concerned with exercising political power than growing in faithfulness. These are easy traps to fall into—ones that the contemporary church itself has not completely escaped. If the faith community or any expression of it follows the lead of Jesus, it can anticipate both challenge and ridicule by those within the structures it challenges and seeks to transform.

The church that serves as yeast will be small (perhaps unnoticeable); it will have a transforming (corrupting) presence in the world as it is; and it will be seen as a threat to the traditions and practices that many hold dear in their lives and faith. Such is the nature of God's work.

A Time-Consuming Process of Change

There is one more insight that comes from the yeast metaphor: Yeast takes time to do its work. It takes time to transform the flour. It takes time to impact what is in order for it to become something different. Leavening is a time-consuming process, one that requires patience. It is also a process that requires a hopeful confidence that something so small, that seems at first to have no significant influence, eventually brings profound change. The church that functions as yeast will need similar patience and confidence in its work.

Matthew's gospel envisioned a church that functioned in the same way as yeast. In doing that Matthew also provided a vision for what the resurrecting faith community might be about.

By comparison God's reign works over time. In a similar way, it attacks the status quo. In doing transformative work, it shows that conventional life under imperial rule is unacceptable. God's ways are not human ways. God's empire is not the same as oppressive, political, socioeconomic, and religious control. So Jesus heals the sick, casts out demons, eats with tax collectors and sinners, urges mercy, promotes access to shared resources, and constitutes alternative households. This is corrupting work in relation to the empire's status quo because it replaces an unjust hierarchical system that furthers the interests of the elite at the expense of the rest. But if a person is well adjusted to a sick society, corrupting is the only path to wholeness. In such a context, to be corrupted is to be transformed, saved, in encountering God's empire, in anticipation of its eventual completion in establishing God's life-giving reign over all things.[6]

Questions for Reflection:

- The Parable of Yeast suggests the following possibilities for the resurrecting faith community: it will be small; it will have a transforming (corrupting) presence in the world as it is; it will be seen as a threat to and a corruption of what many hold dear in their lives and faith; its work will take time and require great patience. How do you respond to these as descriptors of church? Are there some you would reject?
- What additional insights do you see from the parable?
- How might these insights be useful to your congregation?

We said above that no one can know the exact form the church will take, but it is possible to imagine qualities it might have. We believe that, to be about its mission, the resurrecting church will need to ground itself in the love of God and be guided by the way of Jesus. It will need to nurture its spiritual life and claim the ethic of Jesus as its own. We'll look now at some ways these might happen.

NURTURING SPIRITUALITY

Letting go of the ways of the world is impossible in the absence of a spirituality that is deep enough to allow us to embrace the Christ in us and in others. Without that, any faith community will be captive to an array of worldly concerns, from personal morality to social action. Each of these has its place, but without grounding in a deep and genuine spirituality they inevitably become ends in themselves that distract from a focus on the reign of God. Personal morality can become legalistic and too often rely on a God who is about little more than condemning specific behavior. Social action can become a political program all too often aligned with one or another political platform, party, or movement. A community of faith with a focus on personal and corporate spirituality can help counteract these distractions.

The world is a noisy place! There are eight billion people on the planet, and we are all trying to survive, find meaning, and prove our worth to ourselves and to one another. Life as we have configured it, especially in the West, has too often become impersonal and complicated. The pace of living for many is forcing them to multitask, to race from meeting to meeting and crisis to crisis. For others the struggle to survive, to provide the basic necessities of food, shelter, and security is all-consuming. The twenty-four-hour news cycle breeds anxiety, frustration, and anger. Advertisers tell us how unworthy we are unless we live a certain way, buy certain goods, and hold certain values. We are creatures attuned to potential threats to our well-being, a predisposition that has enabled us to survive and evolve over the millennia but hasn't done much to inspire trust in a loving God who knows us deeply and is forever seeking us. One of the challenges of the resurrecting faith community will be to counteract all of this. To do that it will need to develop not just a personal but also a communal spirituality to recapture a deeper spiritual focus. Thankfully, there is already a growing awareness and practice of spiritual disciplines that enable us to enhance our relationship with God and open ourselves to hearing God's word for us. Contemplative prayer, meditation, walking the labyrinth, fasting, spiritual direction, and other disciplines are finding a renewed place and having both a personal and communal impact. Our focus will be on communal spirituality because we are discussing the resurrecting faith community as a whole. Also, deeper personal spirituality is often the result of participation in expressions of communal spirituality.

Communal spiritual discernment, by definition, is carried out by a community of people who have gathered together in a specific context to seek God through their willingness to surrender those things that are creating barriers to their relationship with one another and with God. So people need to be willing to cede their own agendas, their egoism, and their own narrow view of God in order to hear the Spirit at work in the whole body. This means acknowledging their emotional attachments and addiction to a self-image that is more rooted in how the world views success than how God views faithfulness. In the words of the late Jesuit academic Richard Hauser, "The goal of the spiritual life is to allow the Spirit of Christ to influence all our activity, prayer as well as service. Our role in this process is to provide conditions in our lives to enable us to live in tune with [Christ's] Spirit."[7]

This was a primary objective of the spirituality of the desert fathers and mothers, as Anselm Gruen, a German Benedictine monk, explains in his book, *Heaven Begins Within You:*

> Spirituality from below points out that we come to God through careful self-observation and sincere self-knowledge. We don't find out what God wants from us in the lofty ideals we set for ourselves. Often these are merely the expression of our ambition. . . . Spirituality from below thinks that we can discover God's will for us, that we can find our vocation, only if we have the courage to descend into our reality and deal with our passions, our drives, our needs and wishes.

> The way to God leads through our weaknesses and powerlessness. When we are stripped of all power we discover what God has in mind for us, what God can make of us when God fills us completely with divine grace.[8]

The sad truth is that all too often in far too many congregations a focus on communal spiritual life is thwarted by a myriad of other activities in which the congregation is engaged. From board and committee meetings, to running the Sunday school, to planning and executing a wide variety of programs, those involved in the church have little time left for attending to their spiritual lives. And so they burn out, they become frustrated, and, in many cases, once they have fulfilled their obligations, they leave the church altogether.

The commitment that is needed to develop a meaningful spiritual life is a significant one. In truth there are not many people who are both willing and able to take it on. This is yet another reason why the church that is becoming will be small. If the development of a meaningful and deep corporate spirituality is the expectation for a group, it will most likely be small.

In the resurrecting faith community the development of an enduring communal spirituality will be a central focus. In its ministry it will provide the means for developing a deeper awareness of the presence and leading of God in personal and corporate life. After going to a thoroughly uninspiring worship service while on vacation, listening to the homilist blame the members of the congregation for the lack of attendees that day, Dave took these notes: "It seems that these clergy might be so disengaged from the reality of the world that they are not capable of engaging it in a theological manner, which, ironically, the clergy are trained to do. We have failed God and God's people by being preoccupied by all the wrong things and covering it up with an outdated church language that is often meant to inspire guilt rather than joy. In truth, the church exists for two reasons: to seek the divine and understand how that relationship might impact the values and choices we make for ourselves and for others and to bring people together into a community for fellowship and support in this endeavor. This is it." This is what the faith community that is becoming will seek to be and do.

As we engage in this attempt to develop a communal spirituality, we have an array of resources from our faith tradition to draw on. Some of these spiritual practices have been developed and used for communal discernment for centuries. Others of them, however, have most often been associated with an individual's spiritual practice. We believe, however, that they can be expanded for communal discernment purposes.

The Examen Prayer

The Examen has been an integral part of Jesuit practice for centuries. In the mid-sixteenth century, St. Ignatius of Loyola, founder of the Society of Jesus, understood the Examen Prayer as one of the more important exercises necessary to the spiritual life. In the prayer an individual or small group calls for the presence of God and in that presence looks at their experiences during that day, considering what brought them consolation or a sense of joy and what brought them desolation or a sense of failure. They then reflect on where they felt God's presence was revealed in the midst of those experiences.

The Examen Prayer is about awareness and vigilance, which can free us from our own ego needs and desires. In order for us to understand what God is about, to form a connection with God, we first must understand what we are about: What drives us? What motivates us? What are we seeking and why are we seeking it? The late Anthony De Mello, Jesuit priest and psychotherapist, wrote, "The first step in getting control so as not to be pushed around is to become aware. Oh, the painstaking process of coming home, of being aware of what is going on! Where are these drives coming from? Who is pushing me (us)? There is no substitute for this awareness."[9]

Furthermore, when we become aware of what is pushing us and motivating us, then we have a shot of being freed from the compulsions that arise when we live in an unexamined way. It is important to make clear that the Examen is not the least bit helpful for an individual or a community if it leads to self-criticism or guilt. The point of becoming aware is to get to the truth. Understanding the truth about ourselves and our community is the first step in becoming aware of God and what God is up to in our world. We cannot begin from an illusion about ourselves or the world because it will taint our view of God and how we understand the will of God in our context. So, the Examen can only be done from a posture of complete surrender and the desire to be freed from the compulsions that have driven the church for millennia.

A few years ago, Jeff and his wife, Judy, went to a Mark Rothko exhibit at the Museum of Fine Arts in Boston. Jeff was not impressed, at least not initially. Here's his memory of that experience:

> We walked into the exhibit hall and there, hung on the wall in front of me, was a large black painting. It looked as though all Rothko had done was take a can of black paint and slap it on a canvas. I made some disparaging comment about being able to do that myself and maybe then I could get into a museum. Judy, who is a fiber artist with a great awareness of color, told me to just stand there and look at the painting for a few minutes. Being

an obedient husband, that's what I did. And within those few minutes an amazing transformation took place. I began to see in a different way. Hints of color and texture began to appear. There were reds in that black. And there were greens. There was a depth to the way the paint had been applied providing an even greater array of tones. What looked at first glance like a solid sheet of black, was really a wondrous revelation of subtle color, tone, and depth.

As I have pondered this experience, I've come to realize that this is what the Examen is all about. We look at an experience that may seem plain and straightforward, just a typical experience in a typical day—nothing special at all. But when we slow down, when we take the time to look, we see more. We see a depth and richness we hadn't seen before. We see a meaning that we hadn't been aware of before. And in that we may well see the working and the wonder of God.

As those in a faith community gather to examine their life together and engage in the Examen, the following process may be helpful:

- Invite the Spirit's presence and allow time for silence.
- Consider the following questions, allowing time for both discussion and silence.
- What is there to be grateful for in our life together?
- Where do we see God at work in our faith community and the world?
- Where or how have we fallen short as a community of faith?
- Reflect on the insights gained from this experience and consider ways in which group members may begin to live them out.[10]

The Rule of Life

The rise of monastic communities came about as the result of the Roman Empire's fall into the chaos that preceded its demise, taking along with it the Imperial Christianity that sprang up after the Edict of Milan in 313. As the social, cultural, and political props that had legitimized Christianity from the time of Constantine began to lose their influence, the struggling church needed to find stability and a new center to wait out the storm. The monastic community was one such place of refuge. Though traditional monastic communities are struggling today, intentional nontraditional and virtual communities are springing up in many places. What characterizes these communities of faith is the desire to live by a rule of life, a spiritual practice that emerged with the Rule of St. Benedict in the early sixth century CE and one that can be an important dimension of the resurrecting church. The Benedictine monks live, pray, and work together. They believe in working a full day but interrupt their labor with set times for prayer. They take vows to be in relationship with one another and obey their superior, to live a more faithful life, and to provide stability for their monastic community. Today there are many variations on this ancient practice. Some traditional monastic orders offer opportunities for people living in a "secular" context to be associated with them and live out a rule of life in a context very different from traditional monks. These people are called oblates in the Benedictine tradition.

We wonder if, just as the church needed the early monastic communities to provide a refuge from the chaos that surrounded the demise of the Roman Empire, the practice of a rule of life will enable the resurrecting church to discover its identity during this time of disruption and reformation, as the demise of Christendom forces the church today to find stability and a new center. In the words of Dietrich Bonhoeffer, "The renewal of the Church will come from a new type of monasticism which only has in common with the old an uncompromising allegiance to the Sermon on the Mount. It is high time people banded together to do this."[11]

Living in community with people from all walks of life and cultural expressions is a difficult task even for those who have similar religious practices and beliefs. To foster a greater sense of community amidst this diversity, some faith communities have created a community rule of life and invited their congregants to live into and follow this rule and develop a personal rule of life to enhance it. What is a community rule of life?

Simply put, it is a written set of principles that express the priorities of a Christian way of living. The rule is not an end in and of itself but rather a means to strengthen the community's relationship with God, with one another, and with its neighbors. The rule is a way to develop the strengths of the community and challenge its weaknesses. It serves as a framework to keep the community "on track" when the pull of cultural demands becomes oppressive. Here is an annotated example of a community rule of life that comes from The Order of St. Patrick, a "fellowship of Christian clergy and lay contemplatives who wish to dedicate themselves to a secularly cloistered monastic life."[12]

Rule #1: Our Guide is Christ. We shall seek to be formed in Christ's image. This rule serves as the foundation for all of our rules. . . . The Order of St. Patrick serves as a community of like-minded people, upholding one another on the journey of growing in deep, intimate, and meaningful relationship with God.

Rule #2: We shall pray daily. Morning (laud), noon (sext), evening (vespers), and night (compline) prayers shall be observed by each member of the Order. . . . We affirm and believe that prayer allows us access to the power of the Holy Spirit. Through the divine presence of that Holy Spirit, we find and rediscover the strength to grow fully into the image of Christ.

Rule #3: Our cloister is our local church or abbey. Each member shall actively participate in the positive development of the local church or abbey to which they belong.

Rule #4: We shall be faithful stewards. Our stewardship of the good gifts that God has entrusted to us for a time is the expression of our Christian ministry as it relates to Creation.

Rule #5: Our service is our gratitude. . . . Each day, each member of our Order shall seek to perform at least one act of service that flows from that member's genuine gratitude for God's love.

Rule #6: We shall read from the Bible daily. We shall open ourselves to the Holy Scriptures to be formed in the image of Christ.

Rule #7: We shall bring light to the darkness as God has gifted us. We are committed to bringing light into the dark places of life in this world.

Those wishing to live within the parameters of a community rule of life may be encouraged to develop a personal rule of life as a way to enhance the whole. A personal rule of life may tailor the framework and guidelines of the community rule of life to fit an individual's personal context.

Spiritual Direction

Spiritual direction is an art form that has been around since the desert fathers and mothers of the late third and early fourth centuries. A spiritual director is a spiritual companion, helping directees see where the Spirit of God might be moving in their lives. Spiritual direction is often done one-on-one, but group spiritual direction is a practice that has proven to be a deeply enriching experience for many individuals and congregations. If people are vulnerable with one another in a safe environment, then group discernment can often become quite a profound experience for everybody in the group. The first and second examples we offer focus on an overall discussion of communal life; the third example focuses on specific concerns or issues within the life of the community.

The first form is more about observing the path the community is on rather than finding the answer to a specific concern; it is more about the process than the conclusion. A facilitator of this form of group spiritual direction needs to be gifted in the art of observation and have good listening skills. They might begin by asking a probing question to help the group form a picture of the faith community in which they participate.

One model of group spiritual direction, developed by Brother Jack Mostyn CFC, is called Friends of the Mystery and goes something like this: A facilitator is chosen beforehand. No special training is necessary for this task, just somebody with the gifts we described above.

- As the people gather they begin with a time for "check in," asking each person to share a sentence or two about how they are at that time. Request that each person keep it brief.
- The facilitator then calls for a ten-minute period of silence in which individuals are invited to reflect on four aspects of their lives: their inner life, their interpersonal relationships, the structures/organizations they are a part of, and their relationship with nature and the environment.
- The facilitator ends the silence with a few words inviting the group to talk about how God has been present in their lives. Everyone who wishes shares in turn. There is no interrupting or interjecting allowed during this time of sharing. This may go on for an hour or longer if necessary.
- When the facilitator senses that everyone is finished, he or she asks the group for another short time of silence. The facilitator then asks each person what the experience of sharing was like for them. Each person offers a word or phrase, not a long explanation, describing how they are feeling after sharing.
- Then the facilitator poses the question to the whole group: How has the mystery of God been present in this sharing here and now? Each person describes what touched them in the gathering. During this time, dialogue and cross talk is encouraged. Group members are encouraged to think about any theme that may have emerged in the sharing. If an insight, spiritual principle, or truth statement emerges from the conversation, take time to savor and enjoy it.
- The facilitator says a short prayer, and the group decides on the time, place, and facilitator for the next meeting.

A second example of group spiritual direction treats the entire group that is gathered as a "directee." Groups, much like individuals, have personalities and a call from God. In this type of direction, the facilitator is brought on by a board, committee, order, congregation, or other group to do the following.

- Assess the group as it gathers and notice by the way the group interacts, where its life and energy is and where it is not. Reflect this back to the group and allow the group to determine how to use that information in discernment.

- Assess where the Spirit of God as well as "other spirits" are evident. Point this out to the group.

- Gently probe the group with honest, open-ended questions to help it identify where God may be leading at the moment.

- Potentially assist the group in a discernment process.

- Assist the group in doing its business in a more spiritually aware, contemplative manner.

- Assist the group in figuring out how to incorporate the facilitator's observations and reflections into the workings of the group.

- Finally, lead in a time of prayer or other spiritual exercise.

The facilitator observes the group dynamics, including body language and temperament, as the meeting progresses. At the end of each meeting, the facilitator might offer feedback on what was observed during the discussion and insight as to the path the group believes the community is on. Ultimately, over time the facilitator might begin the meeting with a question that leads the group to discern what the next right thing for the community might be, perhaps using a question such as, "What is God up to and how do we get on board?"

Another form of communal spiritual direction is the process of the clearness committee. Seventeenth-century Quakers developed the clearness committee as "a way to draw on both inner and communal resources to deal with personal problems because they had no clerical leaders to 'solve' their problems for them." Parker Palmer describes the purpose of the clearness committee this way:

Behind the Clearness Committee is a simple but crucial conviction: each of us has an inner teacher, a voice of truth, that offers the guidance and power we need to deal with our problems. But that inner voice is often garbled by various kinds of inward and outward interference. The function of the Clearness Committee is not to give advice or "fix" people from the outside in but rather to help people from the inside out.[13]

The committee meets at the invitation of the focus person, who has a problem or concern they would like to address. When it meets, the committee organizes itself by selecting a facilitator and a recorder. The person who is the focus of the meeting presents a specific concern or problem. The members then offer questions intended to help the person sort through issues related to the concern and remove the interference that keeps them from hearing their inner voice. Questions that offer a disguised suggestion—such as "Have you ever thought about doing . . . ?"—are to be avoided. A good question does not have an obvious answer but will help the person see additional dimensions of the concern and begin to look at it from new perspectives. Some questions might invite the person to consider the relationship of the concern to past experiences and feelings. Others might seek to relate the concern to a biblical or faith perspective. The focus person responds to each question as it is asked, offering as much as they are comfortable doing. At the conclusion of the meeting the focus person can make whatever summary comments they wish and is given the recorder's notes for further reflection.

Although originally focused on the concern of an individual, the principles of the clearness committee can be adapted for use in a communal setting. The committee would select a facilitator and a recorder and one person would volunteer to bring the concern to the group, acting on behalf of the group. He or she would offer their understanding of the concern, attempting to describe its presence in and impact on the life of the community. After this, group members would, as in the individual clearness committee, ask questions intended to help sort through the issues related to this concern and develop new insights and perspectives. In this role they are freed from thinking about possible answers and can focus on questions that might reveal different dimensions of the situation they are discussing. In the communal clearness committee experience, although the individual who presented the concern responds to the questions, the learning that takes place is for the entire group. As this process concludes, the members of the group hear a report from the recorder and reflect together on insights they have gained, exploring new understandings and their implications for the decisions that need to be made. Finally, the group can consider whether this process has led them to a point at which a decision can be made that everyone is able to affirm. If this approach is to be taken, it is important to share beforehand the process—especially information about the kinds of questions that are appropriate—so that everyone has an opportunity to buy into the procedure. Without buy-in from everyone, it is best not to take this approach to group decision-making.

We don't engage in group spiritual direction to ask God to solve our problems or give us the answers. We engage in spiritual direction to be in the presence of God and attempt to discern what God is up to in our context. This takes time and a great deal of wrestling with our own values and expectations.

Any number of spiritual exercises or activities may enable this, and what works will likely be different for different people. What matters is not the activity but the way of being that emerges. This is true for both individuals and communities. Whatever form it takes, a focus on group spirituality plays an essential role in opening us to God's presence and activity.

CLAIMING THE ETHIC OF JESUS

Christians, as odd as it may seem, follow a man who said:

- The meek will inherit the earth.
- Love your enemies.
- It is more difficult for a camel to go through the eye of a needle than it is for a rich person to get into heaven.
- Don't worry about what you will eat or wear.
- Hate your mother and father, even life itself.

In a society in which meekness is seen as weakness, enemies are to be defeated, wealth is to be pursued, concern for what one will eat and wear is seen as being responsible, and love of parents and life is expected, it is difficult to figure out just what Jesus had in mind when he said these things. It's no wonder the church has spent great amounts of energy and engaged in great contortions of logic attempting to demonstrate that somehow these words do not apply to those of us who live in this world. We can talk about how Jesus's teaching is the ethic of the kingdom, but not this world; we can explain all about the use of hyperbole in Jesus's teaching; but still the words are right there in front of us. Rather than embrace these words as the words of the One we seek to follow, Christians have more often attempted to rationalize them away. Richard Rohr describes our plight with his characteristic insightfulness:

> Christianity is a bit embarrassed by the powerless one, Jesus. We've made his obvious defeat into a glorious victory. Let's face it, we feel more comfortable with power than with powerlessness and poverty. Who wants to be like Jesus on the cross?
>
> It just doesn't look like a way of influence, a way of access, a way that's going to make any difference in the world. We worship this naked, homeless, bleeding loser, crucified outside the walls of Jerusalem, but we want to be winners.[14]

At a vestry (governing board) meeting one evening, Dave asked the members to envision all the money included in the current parish budget as a pile on the table, then asked "How might God help us to consider ways of using this money to do ministry in our local community that is more meaningful than what we are doing now?" It was difficult for the members of the vestry to even begin to answer that question, for its implications were profound. What would it mean for money now devoted to the building, to the music program, to the staff? How could those possibly be sacrificed? What would it mean for the church that they currently knew? The structural realities of the current situation made it all but impossible to consider what it might mean to spend the money in a different way than it had been spent.

So what is this ethic of Jesus we are to claim as our own? To get at that, let's consider the ministry of Jesus and his proclamation of the coming reign of God. Luke 4:16–21 provides a good beginning point. Carol Lakey Hess notes in her commentary on this text, "If we are going to study, interpret, and follow the gospel, we should keep coming back to this text to measure our work."[15] The chapter begins by recounting the story of Jesus's temptation. Those verses tell us what Jesus *will not* be about in his ministry. Parker Palmer notes in his book *The Active Life* that during this time Jesus rejects four temptations: to prove himself ("if you are the Son of God"), to be relevant by responding to an immediate need rather than focusing on deeper purpose (change stones into bread), to be powerful (worshipping Satan in return for the power Satan says he will give), and to be spectacular (throwing himself down from the pinnacle of the temple).[16] These temptations also confront us, both as individuals and as the church, and quite often we are not as successful as Jesus in resisting them.

The verses that immediately follow the temptation narrative tell us what Jesus *will* be about. They have, in fact, been referred to as the keynote for Jesus's entire ministry.

When he came to Nazareth, where he had been brought up, he went to the synagogue on the sabbath day, as was his custom. He stood up to read, and the scroll of the prophet Isaiah was given to him. He unrolled the scroll and found the place where it was written:

The Spirit of the Lord is upon me,
because he has anointed me
to bring good news to the poor.
He has sent me to proclaim release to the captives
and recovery of sight to the blind,
to let the oppressed go free,
to proclaim the year of the Lord's favor.

And he rolled up the scroll, gave it back to the attendant, and sat down. The eyes of all in the synagogue were fixed on him. Then he began to say to them, "Today this scripture has been fulfilled in your hearing." All spoke well of him and were amazed at the gracious words that came from his mouth. They said, "Is not this Joseph's son?" (Luke 4:16–22)

WHAT JESUS WILL BE ABOUT IS THE POOR, THE CAPTIVE, THE BLIND, and the oppressed. What he will be about is proclaiming the year of the Lord's favor—a reference to the year of Jubilee (Leviticus 25:8–24), when debts are forgiven, slaves are freed, and land returned. While the temptation to spiritualize the words of Jesus is great, they are also a literal expression of his understanding of his ministry. The economic, social, and political implications of these words are profound! That is what his ministry was about. It is the essence of the ethic of Jesus.

If we look more broadly at the ministry of Jesus, we see the words of Luke 4 affirmed in both his words and actions:

- Jesus rejected a religious establishment more concerned about its practices than God's mission, calling its leaders hypocrites and blind guides (Matthew 21)

- Jesus called for a more vital, more vibrant form of faith, asking people to reject what they have been taught and do something radically different (Matthew 5)

- Jesus recognized that correct cultic practice is not the ultimate purpose of religion, criticizing the religious leaders' focus on the minute details of the law while ignoring the weightier matters of justice, mercy, and faith (Matthew 23)

- Jesus understood the reality of institutional demise, predicting the destruction of the temple (Matthew 24)

- Jesus understood that the key to true greatness was servanthood (Mark 10)

- Jesus identified himself with the hungry, the thirsty, the stranger, the naked, the sick, and the prisoner (Matthew 25)

In *The Time Is Now* Joan Chittister makes the prophetic commitment of Jesus clear:

> Jesus . . . moved with drunkards and sinners. He healed the outcast and the enemy. He gathered women as well as men to his side. He chastised leaders who overlooked the poor; he defied the doctrine of sexism that religions use to make male ministers superior, powerful, primary. He stood up and in a clear voice declared wrong any policies of either sacred or secular—church or state—that burdened the backs of the powerless and rushed the spirits of the poor.[17]

Our first step in claiming the ethic of Jesus as our own is to admit that his ethic is not the ethic many Christians have followed. Stories, such as the deceitfulness of Ananias and Sapphira (Acts 5:1–11), make it clear that this was true even in the early church. With the dawn of Christendom, the temptation to abandon this ethic became even stronger. By the end of the fourth century, continuing decrees of successive emperors outlawed paganism and established the Christian faith as the faith of the empire. This change had a profound impact on the church. What had once been a group of mostly poor outsiders was now a group dominated by influential insiders. No longer persecuted, the church had become powerful. The changes in social, cultural, and political status also changed the way in which the gospel was interpreted and the faith was practiced. Worship moved from the catacombs to the basilica. A hierarchy patterned after the structure of the Roman army was established. In art Christ was no longer depicted as the servant but as the victor. The church was given the right to conduct trials. "The new privileges, prestige and power now granted to church leaders soon led to acts of arrogance and even to corruption. . . . As bishops came to have judicial powers, bribes were offered, and often accepted."[18]

The age of Christendom had begun. With few exceptions, the ethic of the Empire had replaced the ethic of Jesus. Status, influence, and power—rather than poverty, humility, and suffering—were the marks of the church. "The Christian church became the established religion of the empire and started reading the Gospel from the position of maintaining power and social order instead of experiencing *the profound power of powerlessness that Jesus revealed.*"[19]

These fourth-century changes and the ways of being church they led to were never faithful to the ethic of Jesus. Now that Christendom no longer shapes the social, political, and cultural context in which the church finds itself, their inappropriateness has become even more apparent. This offers an opportunity to consider in a new way the meaning of the ministry and teaching of Jesus for the church free from the Christendom perspective that has shaped the church's thinking for 1,700 years. It gives the opportunity to nurture the thin thread of commitment to the ethic of Jesus that has been a part of the church from the beginning. For despite all the diversions and digressions, this commitment never went away. There were always those who held and lived by it and passed it on to others.

So, then, what does it mean for the faith community to claim (or perhaps we should say reclaim) the ethic of Jesus? The ethic of Jesus is not about ideology, political orientation, or social policy. Certainly, there are implications for each of these, but it is not primarily about them. Rather, it is about a way of being in a loving relationship with others and the world. Neither is it primarily about critiquing the way things are as much as it is about beginning to live in another way. It provides a place to live out of, not to argue from. It is not so much about others and what they are doing as it is about us and what we are about. As Richard Rohr has often said, "The best criticism of the bad is the practice of the better."[20] Critique has its place, but without this "practice of the better" it easily degenerates into sound and fury, signifying nothing.

The Sermon on the Mount (Matthew 5–7) offers a key for understanding the ethic of Jesus. The study questions we offer focus on what it might mean to live according to the teachings of the Sermon. We want to avoid a more typical response of developing reasons why the teachings might not or cannot apply. If you study these questions, don't be overwhelmed by the entire Sermon. Focus on one portion of it, perhaps even just one verse. Think, pray, and talk together about what it might mean to take that one verse seriously. Here are some questions for you to consider:

- What might it mean to turn the other cheek? (Matthew 5:38–42)
- What would loving your enemies as well as your neighbors look like in your setting? (Matthew 5:43–44)
- How could you live not worrying about what you will wear or what you will eat? (Matthew 6:25–34)
- What would you need to give up, stop doing, start doing; how and when might you do it?
- What support would you need for your attempt?

What is important here is not to develop a complete plan for 100 percent compliance but to determine the steps in the right direction that can be taken and how you will continue to more fully embody the teaching in your lives.

Rustin E. Brian, in *The Death and Resurrection of the Church*, maintains that the church of the future "will look much more like the first few centuries of the church's existence than the last 1,700 years of so." It will "embody the politics of Jesus and his peaceful community."[21]

The church's focus, he says, will interact with and change the culture of the community. It will do this through a variety of strategies depending on the context, resources, and gifts that are available to them. This might include providing support for immigrants and orphans, garden space, a food bank, tutoring, job training, and lawn care for people with physical limitations. Rather than aligning with broader social or political groups, the faith community will find a way to make the ethic of Jesus come alive in its own ministry.

Insight into the ethic of Jesus is provided throughout the New Testament. There is no reason to be unclear about what the ethic is. The struggle comes in our willingness and ability to take it seriously.

There is another dimension to this discussion of claiming the ethic of Jesus that we need to consider.

He [Jesus] said to them, "Doubtless you will quote to me this proverb, 'Doctor, cure yourself!' And you will say, 'Do here also in your hometown the things that we have heard you did at Capernaum.'" And he said, "Truly I tell you, no prophet is accepted in the prophet's hometown. But the truth is, there were many widows in Israel in the time of Elijah, when the heaven was shut up three years and six months, and there was a severe famine over all the land; yet Elijah was sent to none of them except to a widow at Zarephath in Sidon. There were also many lepers in Israel in the time of the prophet Elisha, and none of them was cleansed except Naaman the Syrian." When they heard this, all in the synagogue were filled with rage. They got up, drove him out of the town, and led him to the brow of the hill on which their town was built, so that they might hurl him off the cliff. But he passed through the midst of them and went on his way. (Luke 4:23–30)

Practicing the ethic of Jesus can get you into trouble. In this passage Jesus confronted his listeners with the practical implications of the words he had just read. They had initially heard them as nice words from scripture, offering comfort and assurance, and they liked knowing that they would indeed be fulfilled. But when Jesus began to talk about the practical meaning of that fulfillment, they were offended. They were angered to the point of wanting to do away with Jesus and his message altogether. There is a lesson in this for us. As we move to live more fully into the ethic of Jesus, we will most likely encounter a similar response. We will be challenging the usual and customary ways of thinking and doing. That challenge will in some cases be seen by some as unpatriotic, as disrespectful to the flag, as a criticism of our economic system and a risk to corporate profits, as politically incorrect, as a threat to family values or Second Amendment rights. And when it is seen in any of these ways, the reaction may well be as harsh as the one that Jesus received.

We sense there is little doubt that in claiming the ethic of Jesus we will struggle and perhaps suffer. This is not a pleasant prospect. Most of us seek to avoid, not provoke, struggle and suffering. And yet, these have often been a reality of Christian witness, for that witness is about challenging existing loyalties, perceived security, and the accepted way of doing things.

As much as we seek to avoid struggle and suffering, we are continually confronted not just with their presence in the life of faith but also their redemptive value—their ability to lead us to deeper faith and a more intimate relationship with God. We don't want to sugarcoat the reality of struggle and suffering, but we do believe that if we respond to that reality confident in God's presence and love, it can lead us to a greater love than we would otherwise know. Joan Chittister in her book *Scarred by Struggle, Transformed by Hope* provides an important insight for us:

> To struggle is to begin to see the world differently. It gives us a new sense of self. It tests all the faith in the goodness of God that we have ever professed. It requires an audacity we did not know we had. It demands commitment to the truth. It leads to self-knowledge. It builds forbearance. It tests our purity of heart. It brings total metamorphosis of the soul. If we are willing to persevere through the depths of struggle we can emerge with . . . a kind of personal growth that takes us beyond the pain to understanding. Enduring struggle is the price to be paid for becoming everything we are meant to be in the world.[22]

As we consider the reality of struggle and suffering, it is important to note that many Christendom congregations have made significant efforts to avoid controversy to maintain a sense of community. This is laudable in many ways as it can be a demonstration of love and acceptance. It has had a downside, however. In many cases it has resulted in an avoidance of potentially controversial issues. It has, all too often, resulted in silence when the need for a gospel word was great. Too often this fear of conflict has resulted in congregations such as that in Laodicea: "I [the Son of Man] know your works. You are neither cold nor hot. I wish that you were either cold or hot. So, because you are lukewarm, and neither cold nor hot, I am about to spit you out of my mouth" (Revelation 3:15–16). That is why the faith community that is guided by the image of resurrecting will need to be grounded in a deep spirituality that enables it to discern not a political, economic, or social position but a way of being faithful amidst the political, social, and economic realities in which we are immersed.

This faith community will be discovering a new way of being in the world that is emerging out of Christendom. It will be willing to experiment and at times fail. Those who are a part of this faith community will approach all they do in hope, believing that God is at work in the world and that they can be a part of that work if they are truly open to the leading of the Spirit and have the courage to follow where the Spirit leads.

While in prison during World War II, the year before his execution, Dietrich Bonhoeffer reflected on the state of the church in a world torn apart by war and a country in the throes of totalitarian brutality. His writing is challenging, even painful, to read and yet it is also hopeful. Amazingly it speaks in profound ways to the state of the church today and to the continuing need for a resurrecting church:

> Our church has been fighting during these years only for its self-preservation, as if that were an end in itself. It has become incapable of bringing the word of reconciliation and redemption to humankind and to the world. . . . [We] can be Christians today in only two ways, through prayer and in doing justice among human beings. All Christian thinking, talking and organizing must be born anew, out of that prayer and action. . . . [The church] is still being melted and remolded, and every attempt to help it develop prematurely into a powerful organization again will only delay its conversion and purification. It is not for us to predict the day—but the day will come—when people will once more be called to speak the word of God in such a way that the world is changed and renewed. . . . Until then the Christian cause will be a quiet and hidden one, but there will be people who pray and do justice and wait for God's own time. May you be one of them, and may it be said of you one day: "The path of the righteous is like the light of dawn, which shines brighter and brighter until day." (Proverbs 4:18)[23]

NOTES

1. Warren Carter, "Matthew 13:31–33, 44–52 Commentary by Warren Carter," Sermons and Biblical Studies, Biblia Work, https://www.biblia.work/sermons/matthew-1331-33-44-52-commentary-by-warren-carter/.

2. Joan Chittister, *The Time Is Now: A Call to Uncommon Courage* (New York: Convergent, 2019), 38.

3. Gary Peluso-Verdend, "Matthew 13:31–33, 44–52, Theological Perspective," in *Feasting on the Word, Year A, Volume 3*, edited by David L. Bartlett and Barbara Brown Taylor (Louisville: Westminster John Knox, 2011), 286.

4. Warren Carter, *Matthew and the Margins: A Sociopolitical and Religious Reading* (Maryknoll, NY: Orbis, 2000), 47.

5. Carter, *Matthew and the Margins*, 284.

6. Carter, *Matthew and the Margins*, 291.

7. Richard J. Hauser, *In His Spirit: A Guide to Today's Spirituality* (Boston: Beacon, 2011), 133–34. Quoted in Richard Rohr's Daily Meditation, "Indwelling Spirit," May 24, 2019.

8. Anselm Gruen, *Heaven Begins Within You: Wisdom from the Desert Fathers*, translated by Peter Heinegg (New York: Crossroad, 1999), 24.

9. Anthony De Mello, *Seek God Everywhere: Reflections on the Spiritual Exercises of St. Ignatius*, edited by Gerald O'Collins, Daniel Kendall, and Jeffrey LaBelle (New York: Image/Doubleday, 2010), 43.

10. Adapted from Jim Manney, *A Simple Life-Changing Prayer* (Chicago: Loyola, 2011), 1.

11. Northumbrian Community, *Celtic Daily Prayer* (New York: HarperOne, 2002), 8.

12. "The Order of St. Patrick," https://orderofstpatrick.org/an-explanation-of-the-rules-of-our-order./.

13. Rachel Livsey and Parker Palmer, *The Courage to Teach: A Guide for Reflection and Renewal* (San Francisco: Jossey-Bass, 1999), 43.

14. Richard Rohr, "Changing Sides," Richard Rohr's Daily Meditation, July 4, 2018, https://cac.org/daily-meditations/changing-sides-2018-07-04.

15. Carol Lakey Hess, "Luke 4:14–21, Theological Perspective," in *Feasting on the Word, Year C, Volume 1*, edited by David L. Bartlett and Barbara Brown Taylor (Louisville: Westminster John Knox, 2009), 286.

16. Parker Palmer, *The Active Life: A Spirituality of Work, Creativity, and Caring* (San Francisco: HarperCollins, 1990), 99–119.

17. Chittister, *The Time Is Now*, 43.

18. Justo L. Gonzalez, *The Story of Christianity, Volume 1* (New York: HarperCollins, 2010), 143.

19. Richard Rohr, "From Bottom to Top," Richard Rohr's Daily Medication, Tuesday, April 28, 2015, https://cac.org/daily-meditations/from-bottom-to-top-2015-04-28.

20. "The Eight Core Principles of the Center for Action and Contemplation," https://cac.org/about/the-eight-core-principles/.

21. Rustin Brian, *The Death and Resurrection of the Church* (Eugene: Cascade, 2021), 62–63.

22. Joan Chittister, *Scarred by Struggle, Transformed by Hope* (Grand Rapids: Eerdmans, 2003), 338–42.

23. Dietrich Bonhoeffer, *Letters and Papers from Prison* (Minneapolis: Fortress, 2015), 394–95.

A New Model of Leadership

Inwardly Directed and Outwardly Focused

Search me, O God, and know my heart;
test me and know my thoughts.
See if there is any wicked way in me,
and lead me in the way everlasting.

—PSALM 139:23–24

BE PREPARED FOR A DIFFERENT APPROACH TO LEADERSHIP! IN HIS BOOK, *Failure of Nerve*, the late Edwin Friedman, the noted system theorist, stated the need for a different kind of leadership clearly:

> The way out [of the leadership rut] requires shifting our orientation to the way we think about relationships from one that focuses on techniques that motivate others to one that focuses on the leader's own presence and being.[1]

Congregational leaders need a new understanding of their role no matter which formative image is theirs. The traditional approach to leadership will need to be replaced by one that emphasizes personal reflection, as well as organizational concerns. This form of leadership is not so much about knowing the right answers as discovering the right questions and living with those questions. It's not so much about implementing new programs as becoming receptive to the Spirit's leading. It is based in the prayer of the psalmist: "Search me, O God."

LEADING IN A LIMINAL TIME

For insights on an approach to leadership we believe is essential, we turn to Robert Quinn. Quinn, you will remember, is the one who offered the deep change/slow death concept we discussed in chapter 1.

We share Quinn's belief that to lead effectively in today's world we must first look within ourselves. Our ability to lead effectively depends on our own personal spiritual growth. It's not an easy thing to do, but it is essential for meaningful leadership. As Quinn puts it, "The problem is that to grow, to take the journeys on which our growth is predicated, we must confront our own immaturity, selfishness and lack of courage."[2] Margaret Wheatley makes the same point, perhaps even more strongly:

> We can't trust ourselves to be perfect; we can't trust ourselves to be the best at anything; we can't trust ourselves to succeed; we can't trust ourselves to never cause harm and hurt. What we can trust is our disciplined effort to get to know ourselves. We can learn to know our triggers, our habitual reactions, our strengths and weaknesses. All of this is possible—and essential—if we are to lead sanely in the midst of falling-apart craziness.[3]

Doing this, we believe, requires a spiritual process through which we let go of our egos and seek to discover the Christ within (Colossians 1:27). It may seem ironic that we turn to a secular writer to help us explore a spiritual process, but we believe that, in *Change the World: How Ordinary People Can Accomplish Extraordinary Results*, Quinn offers what is essentially a spiritual approach that provides a pathway to more effective and faithful leadership. Quinn writes in secular terms, but we believe he is essentially spiritual. We have made a few adaptations in the "seed thoughts" he provides, but the essence of it comes from his book. They will be our guide as we consider the role of leaders. These "seed thoughts" are the key to the approach to leadership that is needed today:

- Envision the productive community
- Look within
- Embrace the hypocritical self
- Transcend fear
- Embody a vision of the new community
- Disturb the system
- Surrender to the emergent process
- Entice through moral power

This, as you probably noticed, stands in sharp contrast to most approaches to leadership, both secular and religious. Phrases such as sharing a vision, creating a guiding coalition, and developing a strategy are not here. Instead, much of it focuses on personal work that is essential for leaders before they turn their focus to others. We'll look at each of these seed thoughts, explore their implications from a faith perspective, and consider their meaning for leadership in congregations and communities of faith.

Envision the Productive Community

Envisioning the productive community isn't so much about what you want to do as it is about what you want to be. This primary (both in order and importance) seed thought is about envisioning the kind of community you are seeking to become. Quinn describes a productive community by explaining what happens to its participants. People in a productive community share a common purpose and work for the benefit of all. "They tend to become inner directed and outer focused. They tend to be motivated by a calling that they feel deep within."[4] Think about this quotation from a faith perspective. People in a community of faith are inner directed because of the depth of their spiritual lives. They no longer depend upon the approval and affirmation of others or external rewards and accomplishments; they rely on a sense of their unique giftedness and the presence of Christ within. They are outer focused because they know that their gifts are to be used for others, sharing God's love. They are called by God to use their God-given gifts for others; they live as Christ's disciples in the world.

Congregations whose formative images are remembering and letting go may continue in many of their traditional ways. The remembering congregation does so out of fear of losing what it has been. The letting-go congregation does so with a different understanding of its purpose because it has accepted the reality of its death. Both, however, have the potential to be communities that seek to support and care for all who come while at the same time continue to nurture a caring relationship with the world through their outreach. Those in these communities, like those whom Jesus taught and healed, are brought together by the power of the teaching and healing that takes place there and the connectedness they discover with one another through that. Both the remembering and the letting-go congregations, each in their own way, are providing a community and offering ministry. They do so with differing understandings of what they are about, but both can be faithful expressions of God's work in the church and the world.

The resurrecting congregation is also a productive community—a small group of committed disciples, motivated by that commitment to act as yeast in the world. We believe this is what Jesus was about in calling the first disciples. They were a group of kindred spirits with whom he could form a productive community that was inner directed and outer focused and motivated by a calling from deep within. Jesus made the productive community a reality through his relationships within the group of disciples and he also talked about it. In a very real sense, the Sermon on the Mount (Matthew 5–7) is a description of life within this productive community. It is a community that is earnest in prayer (Matthew 6:5–15), seeks to trust in God (Matthew 6:25–33), and avoids judging others (Matthew 7:1–5). It is also a community that understands it is to be both the salt of the earth and a light to the world (Matthew 5:13–16). To be sure, the disciples didn't always succeed in the attempt to be a productive community, but, in striving to be one, they remained attentive to the Spirit at work in their midst, leading them to engagement in the world.

How then does the leader prepare her- or himself to meet the challenge of leadership in a congregation that is facing an array of new realities? The following seed thoughts point the way. They don't tell us how to do it, for each of us needs to determine that for ourselves, but they do offer helpful suggestions for the journey.

Look Within

Looking within focuses us as leaders on discovering the values that are central to our being, helping us make fundamental choices about the way in which those values will shape our living. It is important to note that these values are not ones we aspire to because we believe they *should* be our values. Neither are they imposed on us by others or society. Rather, they are the values that are genuinely ours. Parker Palmer provides an important faith perspective on the reason for this look within: "Vocation does not come from a voice 'out there' calling me to become something I am not. It comes from a voice 'in here' calling me to be the person I was born to be, to fulfill the original selfhood given me at birth by God."[5] The purpose of the look within is to discover this original selfhood.

This is what Jesus was working through as he was being tempted in the wilderness at the beginning of his ministry. It was his time for a deep look within, to discern the call that was his so that he could fulfill the original selfhood given to him by God. In each temptation he was given the opportunity to affirm or deny the values that were central to his identity and purpose. In resisting each temptation, he was gaining clarity regarding what he was not about. This was a difficult struggle, as most looks within are. It is for us, just as it was for Jesus. But it is also an essential part of the journey to meaningful leadership.

Without the self-knowledge that the look within brings, we are subject to an array of external forces that bombard us every day with messages about who we should be like and what we need to do. We are caught in a morass of expectations that are inevitably based on external factors rather than being the person God created us to be. We shape our lives according to these external expectations rather than an inner, deeper reality.

The look within enables us to make the fundamental choice about who we are and what purpose we have in our living. It also enables us to reflect upon what we say and do so that it can be more fully aligned with the fundamental choices we have made. The discussion of the Examen Prayer in chapter 5 is an example of how this look within can be done.

One essential quality that is necessary for this look within is the ability to cultivate inner silence. In the words of Anthony De Mello, "There is only one way for people to confront themselves and that is through silence."[6] On a recent sabbatical, Dave spent over two weeks in silence in an isolated monastery in the desert southwest, living each day with the internal dialogue that is present to all of us. In Dave's words, "I worked the Examen Prayer as Ignatius prescribed it to his followers, twice a day, at noon and at bedtime. It was very difficult for me having no outside distractions to dilute the inner chatter, but in the end I gained a much deeper awareness of my gifts and shortcomings." Cultivating silence is paramount to self-examination, and this takes time.

While the look within involves individual work, most of us cannot do it on our own. We need help. That help can come in any number of ways: A spiritual director, a therapist, a soul friend are all possibilities. But it is important to have someone you trust to be honest and forthright with you on this journey.

Our journey to leadership in this new way, then, begins with a look within. In the following seed thoughts we'll take a look at some of the things we can expect to encounter as we do that looking.

Embrace the Hypocritical Self

No one wants to be seen as a hypocrite. However, all of us have an image of ourselves that at least in some ways stands in contrast to the way we really act. We're only human, after all. Most of the time we are unaware of this discrepancy. In fact, our psyche encourages this unawareness as a way to protect ourselves. We tend to avoid facing those thoughts and actions that run counter to the image we have of ourselves. But face them we must. Actually, not just face, but embrace. That is, accept them as real parts of who we are—something to be admitted and accepted so that we can work to change.

Quinn writes: "As painful as it might be for us to accept, the truth is that we are all hypocrites. And this is information that we either do not know or do not want to know. Why? Because we value control, winning, suppression of negative feelings, and the pursuit of rational objectives, we find ways to neutralize the slightest signal that we might be making a mistake or failing."[7]

Facing hypocrisy, we believe, is what Jesus was getting at as he acknowledged the very human trait of focusing on the faults of others: "You hypocrite, first take the log out of your own eye, and then you will see clearly to take the speck out of your neighbor's eye" (Matthew 7:5).

But Jesus didn't just talk about it, he experienced it. Mark tells the story of Jesus's encounter with the Syrophoenician woman. This is a difficult passage because Jesus doesn't look very good in it.

> From there he set out and went away to the region of Tyre. He entered a house and did not want anyone to know he was there. Yet he could not escape notice, but a woman whose little daughter had an unclean spirit immediately heard about him, and she came and bowed down at his feet . . . ; She begged him to cast the demon out of her daughter. He said to her, "Let the children be fed first, for it is not fair to take the children's food and throw it to the dogs." But she answered him, "Sir even the dogs under the table eat the children's crumbs." (Mark 7:24–30)

To her credit with great humility she challenged Jesus on his understanding. When she did he apparently saw his error and he healed her daughter. As intriguing as this challenge to Jesus was, what intrigues us most about this passage is the context in which Mark places it. It immediately follows a passage in which Jesus challenged the crowd to see where wrong actions come from:

> "Are you so dull?" he asked. "Don't you see that nothing that enters a person from the outside can defile them? . . ." And he said, "It is what comes out of a person that defiles. For it is from within, from the human heart, that evil intentions come. . . . All these evil things come from within and they defile a person." (Luke 7:18–20)

It is hard to read Jesus's encounter with the Syrophoenician woman and not understand that his reaction to her came from within himself. In his encounter with her, Jesus was able to embrace his hypocritical self and further his understanding of his true calling—to serve not just Jews but gentiles as well.

In the challenge that comes as we inevitably face the need for change in our congregations, we must face our hypocrisy, even if it threatens us, even if we would rather avoid it. If there is a gap between our verbal commitment to follow God's lead into the future and our actual willingness to do that, we need to acknowledge it. If we are not able to do this, our efforts to make the needed change will not be effective. We will continue to look for the easy answers in strategies offered by others and continue to try to recover the past that has escaped us. When these easy answers do not bring the hoped-for results, we will become frustrated, begin to feel like failures, seek to blame others, and perhaps even lose hope. When this happens, our need to deny reality will increase because the pain involved in facing our frustrations and failures will increase. Our willingness to embrace our own hypocrisy prepares us to face the realities involved in creating the new forms of church we are seeking.

Transcend Fear

There are many fears we face in our lives. Jeff, despite knowing there is no reason for it, has a great fear of mice. If one appears, he is likely to jump up on the table and shout, "*eeeek!*" More significantly, even though he has lived a good bit of his life on the edge of what other people expect of him, he still fears he may violate the expectations of the people he is seeking to lead to such an extent that they will reject him and that he will be seen as incompetent or uncaring. One of Dave's biggest fears is being perceived by his parishioners as a shirker. In parishes where Dave has served as the rector, he has taken only one day off a week and consistently worked sixty-plus hours a week to "stay ahead" of the criticism. In his words:

> I used to think that if I consistently stayed ahead of what I thought and what I heard the people's expectations were, then I would have the best chance of being accepted by everybody,

including the most demanding parishioners, and not being blindsided. I understand now that this perspective is dangerous. Of course, that strategy didn't work, because it's impossible to be universally accepted, and the threat of being blindsided is always present. But there is something much more sinister at work in this strategy. This fear of not meeting expectations, or the conflict that arises from it, puts the focus not on what the Spirit is doing in the midst of the community but on the most demanding and threatening people in the parish. Such work habits also upset the balance between work, family responsibilities, and self-care, which can lead to unhealthy boundaries and in some cases clergy misconduct.

Every organization has a set of expectations about the ways in which those who participate in it will conduct themselves, along with sanctions for those who violate those expectations. Sometimes they are explicit but often they are implicit and perhaps even unconscious. We all learn that when we participate in a particular organization it is essential to abide by the expectations. Those who violate them will perhaps not be officially shunned, but they will experience the consequences of their actions. For example, people in the organization might be less friendly toward them, or perhaps they will not be asked to serve in positions of leadership and authority. Perhaps they will be seen as troublemakers or as people who have a problem with authority. Perhaps others will look at them as people who must be having personal problems that are influencing their behavior or as people who just don't understand the way things are done. Or perhaps they will be the object of ridicule. In our experience, the power of these expectations is as true in congregational life as it is in other organizations. Jeff remembers one congregation he served in which a woman seeking to be a leader was criticized because "She dresses to call attention to herself"—something that evidently violated the accepted norms.

Many leaders fear violating the accepted institutional norms. This fear can be especially great if we are always seeking to please others or if we have a need for affirmation. You can hear that fear in the joking about what might happen if you said something or did something outside the norm. You can see it in the potent silence that envelops a room when people disagree but say nothing. You can feel it in a haunting sense that there is an elephant in the room that no one is willing to talk about. You can experience it in the steadfast insistence that the emperor really does have clothes!

Our guess is that the reason angels in the Bible so often begin their pronouncements by saying "Do not be afraid" is that they are going to ask a person to do something outside of the usual and customary practice, something that violates community norms and will get them into trouble: to travel to an alien land (Genesis 46:3); to become pregnant by the Holy Spirit (Luke 1:30); to marry the woman you are engaged to even though she is pregnant (Matthew 1:20); to tell your friends that the person they all knew was dead is alive (Matthew 28:5–6); to keep on telling others about God even though you are being persecuted (Acts 18:9–10). When an angel visits, there is every reason to be afraid.

And yet the Bible provides many illustrations of those who faced and overcame their fears. Abraham and Sarah went out not knowing where they were going (Hebrews 11:8). Mary said, "Here am I, the servant of the Lord; let it be with me according to your word" (Luke 1:38). Joseph took Mary as his wife (Matthew 1:24). The women ran to tell the disciples (Luke 24:9). Paul kept preaching.

All of us live with the fear of what might happen if we fail to conform, because belonging is a very basic human need that we do not want to sacrifice. And many of us find much in being a part of a congregation that we value and don't want to jeopardize. So, we toe the line, we live within the norms, to get along we go along. We follow the expectations that prevail and nothing changes. Quinn observes, "Since the external world is always changing, the organization . . . needs to change as well. Yet because we are held back by fear, the opposite tends to happen. Collectives of people do everything they can to preserve what is familiar to them."[8]

This dynamic is especially powerful in congregations whose primary understanding is that they are family, usually meaning "one big happy family." That understanding often carries with it a strong expectation of being nice to one another, of not arguing or even disagreeing, and of keeping secrets that might be embarrassing if they were known. When fear of departing from the familiar prevails, when it shapes the way any organization conducts itself, especially if it is not acknowledged, it is impossible to lead a congregation into a new way of being church.

This means some people need to have the courage to overcome whatever fear they have and begin to live outside of the usual and customary expectations. Quinn advises, "Just as we must embrace our hypocrisy, we must embrace our fears. We need to experience them so that we can know them. We need to contemplate and come to understand them; only then can we begin to outgrow them."[9] Our fear can be significant. It might be a fear of losing friends or creating conflict. It might be a fear of being criticized and ridiculed or of being the subject of parking lot conversations after committee meetings. For those who are employed, it might be the fear of losing their jobs. Looking within to discover a deeper meaning and purpose in order to become inner directed is essential. This is what empowers us to move beyond the fear that forces conformity and denies the possibility of change. Quinn explains:

We [need to] transcend the sanctions of the normalized world. . . . We must be willing, even when the world is seeking to destroy us, to unflinchingly face our fears and honestly ask ourselves why we are afraid. It requires, at all times, that we listen for and obey the voice of our 'own conscience.' It is only then that we become what we know we were meant to be.[10]

Embody a Vision of the New Community

We return now to a focus on the productive community. As church leaders seek to encourage others to a fuller expression of God's call, it is important that they begin to act out of a new understanding, demonstrating what it means to be church in a new form. So, for example, the leaders in a remembering congregation will seek to continue to support those in denial, while at the same time not support the denial. The leaders in a letting-go church will bring hospice insights to bear on decisions the congregation makes. The leaders in a resurrecting community of faith will seek to further the commitment to the ethic of Jesus. It is through the leaders' ability to live out of this new way of being that each congregation can begin to see and act in that new way. This is why embodying a vision of the new way is essential. As some begin to be church in this new way, whether it be moving beyond denial, adopting insights from hospice care, or seeking to be yeast in the world, others may begin to see and understand that this way offers new hope and possibilities for them and become willing to take the leap themselves.

Jesus modeled a new way as he lived and ministered with his disciples. As Quinn points out, Jesus didn't offer them a mission statement or set up a committee to develop a vision. Neither did he attempt to impose some type of mission upon them. He just encouraged them to love one another, even allowing them to fail in doing this at times so they could learn from those failures. First, however, he loved them and others (especially the outcasts and marginalized). He rejected self-interest and embodied a new way of being faithful. There is a real sense in which this can describe his entire ministry. Dining with tax collectors and sinners, healing the sick, casting out demons, welcoming the children were all embodiments of this new way of being faithful.

Paul is often criticized for encouraging others to be like him, to follow his example (e.g., 1 Corinthians 11:1). The assumption of these critics is that Paul was an egotist who believed he had all the right answers. We favor a different interpretation, one in which Paul understood that he was attempting to embody a vision of a new way of living. In doing that he demonstrated a lived faith and became a model for others.

Disturb the System

This may sound like the most challenging seed thought but, in many ways, it is the easiest. If you have implemented the seed thoughts we have already discussed, rest assured that you have already disturbed the system. You have gone against the usual and customary way of doing things; you have challenged at least some of the assumptions that are commonly held; you have failed to meet the expectations people have of how you should think and act.

Whenever we do these things, we create some degree of chaos in the system. We run against the usual expectation about maintaining equilibrium in an organization. Instead, as Quinn explains, we "seek to understand the system deeply and the individuals who are such an integral part of it. Then [we] try to disrupt the system so that participants must step outside their scripts, pay attention to what is happening right now, and engage in new behavior."[11] The chaos that results requires the members of the organization to act in new ways. In a real sense this is what the pandemic did for all of us. Because of the requirements of quarantining and social distancing we were all forced into new behaviors, even ones we could not have imagined just weeks before. This disrupted the system and opened the way for substantive change to take place. People can and do resist and refuse; they settle for the least amount of adaptation that is needed for survival. However, chaos provides a possibility for significant change. The key is to maintain what Quinn calls "bounded instability" or chaos that is significant enough to cause disruption but not so great as to cause system breakdown.

In their book *Leadership on the Line* Ronald Heifetz and Marty Linksy talk about the need to control the temperature. It is their way of saying, "Keep the chaos bounded." Focus on keeping things reasonably disturbed, so there is an itch that must be scratched. The challenge here, of course, is to disturb people about the right things, so that the scratching can be constructive.

Jesus was a great disturber of the system—not because he was an ornery troublemaker but because he was committed to embodying a new way of faithfulness. He dined with tax collectors and sinners. He was critical of the religious establishment. He picked grain on the Sabbath. He told stories that provoked and angered others. All of his provocations challenged the way things were usually done. They disturbed the system that was cherished by the political and religious leaders, a system they were determined to protect at all cost.

As the experience of Jesus demonstrates, challenging the system is risky business. It's the reason Ronald Heifetz and Marty Linsky subtitled their book *Staying Alive through the Dangers of Leading*. Disrupting the system, they note, inevitably means that we open ourselves to being marginalized, diverted, attacked, or seduced.[12] We are only capable of staying with it if we have faced and embraced our fears about each of those possibilities.

Surrender to the Emergent Process

We have been describing a process, but it is not like any other process. It's not a series of steps you move through in order to reach some predetermined outcome. As Quinn describes it, it is more like walking naked into the unknown. Like Abraham and Sarah, we go out not knowing where we are going with nothing but ourselves. Through the previous seed thoughts, we have bared our souls, we have acknowledged our hypocrisy, we have faced our fears. We have talked about the way this inward journey can impact others and the system in which we exist. The process has begun to unfold, but we still do not—still cannot—know precisely where we are going. We cannot, even now, create concrete, specific, and verifiable objectives. We do not know precisely what this new form of church will be. Now is the time we need to surrender to the process so that it can unfold.

This surrender requires trust. Trust in the process. Trust in ourselves. Trust in others. It also requires trust that the Spirit is with you no matter what happens. Quinn describes it as akin to Jesus telling his disciples not to worry when they are handed over to the authorities because "what you are to say will be given to you at that time" (Matthew 10:19). Quinn writes, "Jesus tells his disciples that their behavior will disturb the system and they will be brought to stand before the authority figures. He then advises them to not worry but to trust the process."[13] Jesus offers a profound example of trusting the process, as he travels to Jerusalem and engages in the events of Holy Week. Our trusting of the process may not lead to suffering and death, but it will take us into the unknown and into the possibility of encountering the provocative presence of God in our lives.

Trusting the process is essential for a number of reasons. First, this trust will, as Jesus promised the disciples when he sent them out, help us know what to say. The inner work we have done to this point opens us up to the people and the moment. It enables us to understand those who are with us and to live in that moment with them. If we trust the process, the words will come to help us engage the people and the moment more deeply.

What we are to say will come to us if we do the inner work of the seed thoughts, which will in turn open us to the pain, the struggle, the possibilities, and the hope of our setting and time. Of course, there is no guarantee that even then what we say will impact the thinking of others. The entrenchment, the need to avoid and deny, the desire to keep things as they are or return to the way they were may be too great. That may add to our own pain, struggle, and frustration, but it doesn't stop us from trying if we trust the emergent process.

Trusting the process also means living in the faith that, as Quinn maintains, "when a critical mass of people internalizes a shared mindset, centralized leadership becomes unnecessary. The system will self-organize. This is difficult to comprehend and threatening in its implications."[14] Having faith that the system will self-organize should be celebrated because it gets us off the hook. We, as leaders, don't have to figure it out. We just need not to stand in the way of it happening. But it is also threatening, because it requires us to give up control, to trust the process. Imagine what this faith would do to bylaws and books of order, to plans and procedures, to hierarchical systems of authority and control. It is threatening indeed! And yet, it is what can happen.

While writing this book, Jeff attended a reunion of the youth group he worked with while he was in seminary. This is the way he describes that event and why it was possible:

> I began working with that group fifty years ago. They are all in their mid-sixtiess now. They are scattered around the country. But a large percentage of them came to the reunion. Those who could not attend were deeply missed, even as they missed being there. All this from a group of people who fifty years ago showed up at the church on Sunday evening primarily because they had no place else to go. They were in many ways typical high school students but didn't really fit into any of the usual school cliques. That first year we just existed together. I planned and planned and often got frustrated at the lack of response. But we kept at

it. Sunday night meetings, occasional retreats, and perhaps most importantly, street hockey in the church basement. Those games were fun. Those who were there began to invite friends. Summer came and went; the second year together began. And something happened. They began to sing together. They began to share more deeply with each other. Their innate giftedness emerged. They laughed a lot. But it wasn't always pleasant. I still remember going through weeks of thinking I couldn't do anything right. I continued planning the way I had the first year, but the group resisted and became critical. They no longer seemed to appreciate my work (and I, of course, thought they didn't appreciate me). The patterns of the past needed to change. My practice of making all the major decisions for the group was no longer needed. My need to play this role had become dysfunctional and the others in their resistance were trying to make some important changes. It all came together in my thinking following the Youth Sunday worship service. In my attempt to thank them and tell them how much I appreciated all they had done I actually said, "I want you to know how proud I am of me and what a great job I did." That was when I decided to let go and give up my own ego-based need to control. That was also when the true depth of the group and the people in it began to emerge. They had found a new way of being. They had internalized a mindset. Central leadership was no longer needed. In fact, it would be detrimental. This new way of being developed over their remaining time together. It deepened and grew stronger. And it is certainly one of the reasons that more than fifty years later they still get together to be a true church for each other.

Entice Through Moral Power

Our ability to entice through moral power depends upon our integrity, which in turn depends on continuing to work on our hypocrisy gaps. This returns us to the earlier seed thought of embracing the hypocritical self. We don't need to be perfect, but we do need to recognize and continue to seek to close the gap between the person we profess to be and the person we are. Doing this, in Quinn's view, invites others to do the same, which changes the system.

When we close a hypocrisy gap and begin to live with integrity, Quinn says, "We become more inner directed and other focused. Since we are more aligned with some higher standard, we become a living symbol of that standard and others are able to see what we are about and hopefully desire to join with us. In joining with these others, we become a productive community."[15]

Living with integrity promotes a change in the system because it makes room for others to think and act differently. It changes the nature of our relationship and requires others to pay attention and seek a new way. They can choose what that way will be. Some may choose to resist. Others, however, may be attracted by this new way of being and be more open to change themselves.

Jesus illustrates the use of moral power in his interaction with the woman caught in adultery in John 8. He took the time he needed for reflection in order to ensure that he would not act hypocritically as he did with the Syrophoenician woman, refused to condemn her, and called the crowd's attention to their own hypocrisy by reminding them that they were sinners as well. It worked as none of them threw the first stone.

The closing of our hypocrisy gaps lessens our need to focus on our own ego needs. As that happens it becomes possible for us to demonstrate a concern for the people we are with, whether or not they agree with us on particular issues. We can care about their continued well-being while we continue to work to make the productive community a reality. Our ability to do this has the potential for others to see the value of what we are about, the purpose to which we have committed ourselves.

Strength, Sensitivity, and Faith

We warned you at the beginning of this chapter to prepare for a different kind of leadership. We hope you now understand why we did this. We recognize that in attempting to describe this approach to leadership in writing and within the limits of a book, we have made it sound simpler and easier than it really is—perhaps even facile. But we know the transition in leadership style we advocate can never be an easy one. It takes great personal strength coupled with profound sensitivity to others and deep faith that you are about God's work. This is why the look within and focus on self are essential. It also takes the support and encouragement of those who are seeking a similar way for their lives and who understand that a productive community (a community of faith and practice) is needed to aid them in doing that. It is with them and through them that the Spirit works to transform our personal lives and perhaps also the institutions of which we are a part. There are no guarantees, of course.

NOTES

1. Edwin H. Friedman, *A Failure of Nerve: Leadership in the Age of the Quick Fix* (New York: Seabury, 2007), 4.

2. Robert E. Quinn, *Deep Change: Discovering the Leader Within* (San Francisco: Jossey-Bass, 1996), 37.

3. Margaret Wheatley, *Who Do We Choose to Be? Facing Reality, Claiming Leadership, Restoring Sanity* (Oakland: Berrett-Koehler, 2017), 274.

4. Robert Quinn, *Change the World: How Ordinary People Can Accomplish Extraordinary Results* (San Francisco: Jossey-Bass, 2000), 28

5. Parker Palmer, *Let Your Life Speak: Listening for the Voice of Vocation* (San Francisco: Jossey-Bass, 2000), 10.

6. Anthony De Mello, *Seek God Everywhere: Reflections on the Spiritual Exercises of St. Ignatius,* edited by Gerald O'Collins, Daniel Kendall, and Jeffrey LaBelle (New York: Image/Doubleday, 2010), 1.

7. Quinn, *Change the World,* 75.

8. Quinn, *Change the World,* 113.

9. Quinn, *Change the World,* 99.

10. Quinn, *Change the World,* 117.

11. Quinn, *Change the World,* 162.

12. Ronald A. Heifetz and Marty Linsky, *Leadership on the Line: Staying Alive through the Dangers of Leading* (Boston: Harvard Business School, 2002), 31.

13. Quinn, *Change the World,* 171.

14. Quinn, *Change the World,* 184.

15. Quinn, *Change the World,* 193.

Conclusion

WE HAVE SHARED QUITE A JOURNEY THROUGH THE PAGES OF THIS BOOK.
We hope you have found the trip both interesting and insightful. The challenge for us as people of faith living in a liminal time is a significant one. There are no easy answers. That's why we began the book with a reality check. If we are not willing to face the reality of who we are and what the congregation we are a part of is, if we cannot look honestly at the world we live in and the way the church interacts with that world, we cannot be open to the ways God is at work in the world and calling us to join in.

Our aim in response to the reality the church faces today has been to recognize and affirm three forms of church that are likely to emerge in this liminal time. By its very nature, liminal time requires diverse expressions of church. What has been still has its place, providing important and needed ministry. This is why the images of Remembering and Letting Go provide a way of faithfully shaping a congregation's life and ministry. What is becoming is essential, exploring ways to be church in the changing world in which we live. This is why the image of Resurrecting also provides a way of faithfully shaping life and ministry. All three images offer the possibility of meaningful and faithful ministry in today's world.

While it is important to affirm all three images of church, it is also essential to accept the reality that none of them is perfect or complete. All expressions of these images are challenged to become even more faithful. That, too, has been a part of what we have been about. Each of the chapters on the images provides suggestions for meeting the challenge to greater faithfulness. We hope you have found those suggestions realistic and helpful.

No matter the image, a different kind of leadership is needed for a liminal time. No one knows the answers. No one can be certain of the vision. Preparing to lead in this setting begins with a look within so that the person we offer to others as a leader is aware and able to act with healthy conviction. This is what is necessary to build the trust that is essential for leading into the unknown. It is the one constant in the great variety of expressions of church that exist today.

All three images depend on people of faith faithfully seeking what God is asking of them—what the right thing for them is. Just as certainly, all three depend on the faithfulness of God, who is always at work to bring love to people and the world, even when we are unaware and uncertain.

There are no guarantees, of course. The images have no magical power. The look within can still be faulty. But we believe it is time for at least some of us who have been part of the institutional church to begin this journey to a new way of being for ourselves and for the church we love because it is God's gift to us.

Selected Bibliography

Beaumont, Susan. *How to Lead When You Don't Know Where You're Going: Leading in a Liminal Season*. Lanham, MD: Rowman & Littlefield, 2019.

Bonhoeffer, Dietrich. "Jesus Christ and the Essence of Christianity," in *The Bonhoeffer Reader*, edited by Clifford J. Green and Michael DeJonge. Minneapolis: Fortress, 2013, 68.

———. *Letters and Papers from Prison*. Minneapolis: Fortress, 2015.

Brian, Rustin E. *The Death and Resurrection of the Church*. Eugene: Cascade, 2021.

Brueggemann, Walter. *Cadences of Home: Preaching Among Exiles*. Louisville: Westminster John Knox, 1997.

Callanan, Maggie. *Final Journeys: A Practical Guide for Bringing Care and Comfort at the End of Life*. New York: Bantam, 2009.

Carter, Warren. *Matthew and the Margins: A Sociopolitical and Religious Reading*. Maryknoll, NY: Orbis, 2000.

Chittister, Joan D. *Scarred by Struggle, Transformed by Hope*. Grand Rapids: Eerdmans, 2003.

———. *The Time is Now: A Call to Uncommon Courage*. New York: Convergent, 2019.

Cloud, Henry. *Necessary Endings*. New York: HarperCollins, 2010.

De Mello, Anthony. *Seek God Everywhere: Reflections on the Spiritual Exercises of St. Ignatius*, edited by Gerald O'Collins, Daniel Kendall, and Jeffrey LaBelle. New York: Image/Doubleday, 2010.

Dougherty, Rose Mary. *Group Spiritual Direction: Community for Discernment*. Mahwah, NJ: Paulist, 1995.

Farnham, Suzanne G., Stephanie A. Hull, and R. Taylor McLean. *Grounded in God: Listening Hearts Discernment for Group Deliberations* (revised edition). Harrisburg: Morehouse, 1999.

Farnham, Suzanne G., Joseph P. Gill, R. Taylor McLean, and Susan M. Ward. *Listening Hearts: Discerning Call in Community*. Harrisburg: Morehouse, 1991.

Friedman, Edwin H. *A Failure of Nerve: Leadership in the Age of the Quick Fix*. New York: Seabury, 2007.

Gonzalez, Justo L. *The Story of Christianity, Volume 1*. New York: HarperCollins, 2010.

Gruen, Anselm. *Heaven Begins Within You: Wisdom from the Desert Fathers*, translated by Peter Heinegg. New York: Crossroad, 1999.

Hauser, Richard J. *In His Spirit: A Guide to Today's Spirituality*. Boston: Beacon, 2011.

Heifetz, Ronald A., and Marty Linsky. *Leadership on the Line: Staying Alive through the Dangers of Leading.* Boston: Harvard Business School, 2002.

Jones, Jeffrey D. *Facing Decline, Finding Hope: New Possibilities for Faithful Churches.* Lanham, MD: Rowman & Littlefield, 2015.

Livsey, Rachel, and Parker Palmer. *The Courage to Teach: A Guide for Reflection and Renewal.* San Francisco: Jossey-Bass, 1999.

McLaren, Brian D. *Faith After Doubt: Why Your Beliefs Stopped Working and What to Do About It.* New York: St. Martin's, 2021.

Manney, Jim. *A Simple Life-Changing Prayer.* Chicago: Loyola, 2011.

May, Gerald G. *Addiction and Grace: Love and Spirituality in the Healing of Addictions.* New York: HarperOne, 1988.

Mead, Loren. *The Once and Future Church Collection.* Lanham, MD: Rowman & Littlefield/Alban, 1991.

Merton, Thomas. *The Silent Life.* New York: Farrar, Straus, & Cudahy, 1957.

Morris, Danny E., and Charles M. Olsen. *Discerning God's Will Together: A Spiritual Practice for the Church.* Herndon, VA: Alban, 2012.

Northumbrian Community. *Celtic Daily Prayer.* New York: HarperOne, 2002.

Nouwen, Henri J. M. *Our Greatest Gift: A Meditation on Dying and Caring.* New York: HarperCollins, 1994.

Palmer, Parker J. *The Active Life: A Spirituality of Work, Creativity, and Caring.* San Francisco: HarperCollins, 1990.

———. *Let Your Life Speak: Listening for the Voice of Vocation.* San Francisco: Jossey-Bass, 2000.

Quinn, Robert E. *Change the World: How Ordinary People Can Accomplish Extraordinary Results.* San Francisco: Jossey-Bass, 2000.

———. *Deep Change: Discovering the Leader Within.* San Francisco: Jossey-Bass, 1996.

Rohr, Richard. *Breathing Under Water: Spirituality and the Twelve Steps.* Cincinnati: Franciscan Media, 2011.

Roxburgh, Alan J. *Joining God in the Great Unraveling: Where We Are & What I've Learned.* Eugene: Cascade, 2021.

Schaef, Anne Wilson, and Diane Fassel. *The Addictive Organization: Why We Overwork, Cover Up, Pick Up the Pieces, Please the Boss, and Perpetuate Sick Organizations.* New York: HarperCollins, 1990.

Taylor, Barbara Brown. *Leaving Church: A Memoir of Faith.* San Francisco: HarperCollins, 2006.

Tickle, Phyllis. *The Great Emergence: How Christianity Is Changing and Why.* Grand Rapids: Baker, 2008.

Wheatley, Margaret J. *So Far from Home: Lost and Found in Our Brave New World.* San Francisco: Berrett-Koehler, 2012.

———. *Who Do We Choose to Be? Facing Reality, Claiming Leadership, Restoring Sanity.* Oakland: Berrett-Koehler, 2017.

INDEX

About the Authors

Jeff is the author of a number of books on congregational life and leadership, including: *Traveling Together: A Guide for Disciple-Forming Congregations* (Alban) and *Facing Decline, Finding Hope* (Rowman & Littlefield). He has served as the pastor of three churches, the interim pastor of two churches, and twice as a national staff person for the American Baptist Board of Educational Ministries. He retired as the director of ministerial studies and associate professor of ministerial leadership from Andover Newton Theological School in 2015. He currently lives in Sarasota, Florida, with his wife Judy. They both look forward to and cherish times with their two sons, Chris and Ben, and their families, especially their three grandchildren.

Dave worked in the electrical/communications supply business before entering Princeton Theological Seminary in 1990. He has served as the assistant rector to Trinity Church in Buckingham, Pennsylvania; rector to the Church of the Good Shepherd in Wareham, Massachusetts; rector to Christ Church Parish in Plymouth, Massachusetts; and is currently the priest-in-charge to Zion Episcopal Church in Manchester Center, Vermont. Dave is also an active spiritual director for clergy. Johnna, his wife of twenty-eight years, is a Christian educator and writer. They are the proud parents of two sons, Colin (25) and Jared (21).

Printed in the USA
CPSIA information can be obtained
at www.ICGtesting.com
LVHW041535040524
779351LV00008B/536